Mind over Matter

Mind over Matter

By the Editors of Time-Life Books

TIME-LIFE BOOKS, ALEXANDRIA, VIRGINIA

CONTENTS

CHAPTER 1

Physical Powers of Will

adio listeners who tuned in to the British Broadcasting Corporation's "Jimmy Young Show" on November 22, 1973, knew that something special was in store. Uri Geller, a darkly handsome young nightclub performer from Israel, was to be Young's featured guest on the popular daily program, and the advance billing for the show promised that he would perform patently impossible stunts demonstrating the power of his mind over ordinary objects. But as Geller would report later in an autobiography, even he was surprised at what happened that day.

"Jimmy began with the usual questions," Geller wrote. "He asked when I had first found out that I was able to bend keys, nails or other metal objects just by touching them lightly, and when I had learned I could start up a watch or clock that hadn't run for years. I said I had noticed these things way back in my first years in school, much to the surprise of my classmates, my teachers, my parents—and also myself."

The skeptical Young asked Geller to demonstrate his metal-bending powers. With the host and the studio engineers watching closely, Geller laid one of Young's house keys on the table between them and covered it with his flattened palm. Then, inviting the participation of his radio audience, Geller suggested, "If there are any broken watches in your house, please concentrate on them and try to make them work. Just take them in your hand and concentrate on them."

Scarcely had he finished speaking than Geller raised his hand from the key and the astonished Young exclaimed, "It's bending right in front of me. I can't believe it!" The radio host was eager to know more of Geller's repertoire, and the young psychic went on to describe other feats of metal bending, machine repair, and mental telepathy that he could call upon. While they were talking, the show's producer rushed into the studio and thrust a handful of notes at Young. Minutes later the harried producer returned with more slips of paper, and so it went, with several more interruptions before the show's end. When Young paused to glance at some of the notes, he discovered that frightened, astonished listeners were calling in by the scores to report strange events that had occurred during Geller's performance.

"All England seemed to be bending," Geller later wrote. "Knives, forks, spoons, keys, and nails were bending in homes everywhere, near and far from London. A lady from Harrow reported that she was stirring soup when suddenly the ladle started bending. The gold bracelet of a girl in Surrey buckled and bent. A police constable said that several knives and spoons had curled up. A jeweler reported that half the pieces on a tray of cutlery bent. A watchmaker said that his tweezers had done the same. There were reports of watches and clocks starting up that hadn't run for years."

Soon, Uri Geller's name and his mysterious talents were being touted on the front pages of newspapers and on prime-time television all over the world. The public loved the hoopla, but sober journalists and conservative scientists watched with a jaundiced eye, presuming that Geller was just one more magician whose alleged "gift" would soon be exposed as artifice. The majority of scientists dismissed the strange events as the products of delusion, fraud, coincidence, or known sensory abilities. They roundly rejected any suggestion that Geller's activities could only be explained by new mechanisms or processes. Some cited the so-called law of parsimony, which maintains that known physical laws and one's own reason should always be preferred over exotic theories whenever the simpler, more obvious answers provide an adequate explanation. But do they? Some parapsychologists think not. Having observed Geller in action, they are convinced that that most controversial of paranormal powers, psychokinesis, is a reality, and a number of physicists and psychologists are inclined to agree. Psychokinesis—or PK, as it is commonly known—refers to the alleged ability of the human mind to influence objects and events without the benefit of physical contact with them. Literally translated from its Greek roots, the word psychokinesis means "motion produced by the mind"; in its more popular interpretation, it is nothing less than "mind over matter."

PK can supposedly be directed either consciously or unconsciously, with results that may or may not be obvious to an observer. Some instances of reported PK, like Geller's metal bending and clock starting, are played out on what investigators term a "macro" scale, with their seeming results readily appreciated by the naked eye. According to current theory, another example of macro-PK at work might include poltergeists, those unruly racketing spirits that are believed to erupt in households, causing all manner of noises and hurling objects through the air *(pages 37-55)*. Certain séance effects, such as table tilting, rappings, and materializations have also been interpreted as macro-PK, as have optical effects, such as luminous "spirit lights," and teleportation effects, or the movement of objects into and out of enclosed spaces without visible aid.

Other forms of alleged psychokinesis may be so subtle as to be detectable only in the laboratory, however, by application of statistics or scientific measuring devices or both. Termed "micro-PK," these phenomena include effects on target systems, such as random number or event generators and dice-rolling machines, where results that should conform to the normal laws of probability are thought by some to have been altered significantly by PK. The ability to influence air temperature and magnetic fields and to produce so-called thoughtographs by psychically manipulating the chemical particles on photographic film is also considered an example of micropsychokinesis.

A third, and most intensely personal, form of PK involves the supposed power of the mind over self. This mental mastery of the human body is said to manifest itself in such diverse ways as being able to block out pain, levitate the body, and perform psychic healing, during which positive biochemical changes allegedly take place without conventional medical treatment.

Those who study the field of parapsychology generally regard psychokinesis as related to extrasensory perception, or ESP, the supposed ability to acquire or transmit information through means other than known sensory channels. PK and ESP are often referred to collectively as psi phenomena, or simply psi, after the first letter in the Greek word *psyche,* meaning "mind or spirit." As the professionals explain it, both ESP and PK involve some kind of interaction be-

tween the mind and the material world. ESP, it is said, is a demonstration of a mental exchange with another person's brain or with the physical world; PK is a physical influence. Both forms of psi appear to share a fine disregard for physical barriers of any sort—their energies can reportedly penetrate locked doors and steel walls and travel long distances with no diminution of effect.

But if there is relative agreement in parapsychological circles as to what constitutes psi phenomena, there is nothing but controversy and speculation regarding how any alleged mental force might actually be translated into physical action. Some psi researchers, among them psychologist John Beloff of the University of Edinburgh, contend that PK simply exists. "Under certain conditions, still to be established," Beloff has written, "an idea or intention in the mind can automatically constrain a physical system to act in such a way as to express the idea or intention. That this is, in the last resort, [is] an ultimate fact about the world." Others believe that PK is a type of reordered cosmic energy, a life force that can, at times, be channeled through the human mind. Still others believe that psychokinetic energy is a force within all humankind, just waiting to be tapped. But those speculations and numerous others leave many questions unresolved. And the search for answers, first begun hundreds of

When Uri Geller (right) appeared on European radio and television shows in the early 1970s, claiming to bend metal objects with his mind, hundreds of people in his broadcast audience reported simultaneous effects in their homes. Among them (above, from left), Barbara Scheid of West Germany maintained that her fifty-three-piece silver service had twisted; George Porter of Great Britain allegedly watched several objects curl, including a spoon he was holding; and Dora Portman, a housewife from Harrow, England, claimed that her soup ladle suddenly drooped as she stirred a meal.

years ago, is continued yet to-day—leading to still more speculation, still more questions.

The notion that the mind might have occult influence over matter appears to go far back in human history, though it was apparently not until the seventeenth century that anyone went on record to say that psychokinesis deserved serious philosophic investigation. Sir Francis Bacon, perhaps the greatest intellect of the Elizabethan age and a man singularly devoted to the idea of inductive reasoning and the experimental method, theorized in his 1627 collection of essays, *Sylva Sylvarum: Or a Natural History,* that there may be an occult force within one's being that is capable through the "binding of thoughts" of influencing the material world. He proposed that the existence of this binding force might be tested "upon things that have the lightest and easiest motions," among them the "shuffling of cards, or casting of dice." It was not until the mid-nineteenth century, however, that any consistent efforts were made to explore the truth or falsity behind alleged psi phenomena.

The advent of Spiritualism in the mid-1800s spurred an enormous amount of popular interest in all sorts of psychic mat-

During an attempted levitation in 1938, British medium Colin Evans appears to rise from the floor at a séance in London's darkened Conway Hall. Evans took the photograph himself, activating the flash camera with a switch in the white cord gripped in his left hand.

ters, both in the United States and Europe. This quasi-religious movement held as its fundamental premise that the dead survive discarnate in a world beyond, as spirits or intelligences that are able to communicate with the living through "sensitives," or "mediums." Of particular interest to both scientists and savants were the so-called physical mediums, who reportedly relayed the messages of otherworldly spirits to the living in the form of rappings, table tiltings, or other séance effects.

Not surprisingly, most members of the scientific community were loath to cross the boundary into psychic research. Indeed, the majority of them expressed contempt for—and perhaps some underlying fear of—any phenomena that could not be readily explained by current science. There were some, however, who theorized that the mysterious séance happenings were not signals from the spirit world, but psychokinetic phenomena emanating from the mediums themselves—perhaps produced by the "binding of thoughts," a conscious or subconscious act of will.

One of the first to attempt an in-depth study of such events was the respected British physicist Michael Faraday. In 1853,

Faraday engaged several "successful table-movers" in an investigation of the table-turning effect common at séances. He created a number of ingenious devices that he placed on the tabletop during various experiments; all were designed to reveal whether any table movements were somehow initiated by the object itself or by the sitters. Faraday came away from his efforts convinced that, although the sitters believed themselves to be only pressing down on the tabletop with their fingertips, they were actually unconsciously pushing it in the direction they expected it to rotate.

That same year, a number of European investigators took up the psi challenge, also restricting their examination to such physical séance effects as table movements and levitation. Like Faraday, Count Agénor de Gasparin concluded that the energy evidenced in such maneuvers was neither spiritual in origin nor drawn from some external source. De Gasparin, a Frenchman working in Switzerland, proposed the theory that the energy was the product of a "psychic fluid" present in the bodies of the séance participants and that it could be summoned up only as a conscious act of will. "Without the will we obtain nothing," he said. "We might sit there in chain twenty-four hours in succession without getting the slightest movement."

De Gasparin's conclusions were shared in most respects by Marc Thury, a professor of natural history and astronomy at the Academy of Geneva. In an 1855 book detailing his study of telekinetic phenomena, Thury posed the novel theory that people could also set loose psychic energies from their unconscious. He cited as a particularly dramatic example the case of an eleven-year-old Genevese boy who had been practicing psychokinesis. Over time, according to Thury, the boy's skills improved, but objects then began to move in apparent response to unconscious desires or thoughts. Gradually, he lost all control over his produc-

tion of psychokinesis. For example, his music lessons were repeatedly interrupted by the levitation of his piano. Although others attempted to hold the piano down, Thury stated, it continued to rise.

As some skilled investigators discovered at the time, many of the purported psychics of the golden age of Spiritualism were nothing more than rank charlatans or stage magicians pulling the wool over the eyes of a gullible public. Others, however, demonstrated apparent PK effects that are difficult to explain even today. One of them was the celebrated nineteenth-century sensitive D. D. Home.

For Daniel Dunglas Home (pronounced Hume), acquaintance with the paranormal allegedly came early. Born in Edinburgh in 1833, Home was sent to Connecticut as a baby to live with his aunt and uncle. During his childhood, he reportedly had several psychic experiences, the most compelling occurring at the age of seventeen. Home's emotional bond with his mother was apparently strong, and one night her spirit supposedly appeared to him. "Dan, twelve o'clock," it said, and then disappeared. Home later learned that his mother had died at that very hour. Not long afterward, to the distress of the boy's aunt and uncle, rapping noises commenced throughout the house, and furniture began skittering across the

11

floor. Soon Home was responding with his own raps—communicating, he said, with his mother and with other spirits. Convinced that Home was doing Satan's work, his aunt and uncle soon turned him out of the house for their own safety. But the expulsion evidently proved no hardship. Friends and neighbors were eager to enjoy the benefits of his ever-expanding psychic gifts, which the likable medium willingly provided in exchange for room and board.

Home eventually went on to become the foremost medium of his time, notable both for the fact that he never charged fees for his services and for his ability to produce a remarkable array of psychokinetic phenomena. Along with the usual menu of spirit telegraphs and table tiltings, Home was reported also to produce human levitations *(pages 115-116),* spirit materializations, body elongations, and the playing of the song "Home Sweet Home" on an accordion that was floating several feet beyond his reach.

But even the scientific community could not ignore him for long. When Home was performing in England in 1871, the noted physicist and fellow of the Royal Society, William Crookes, gained his cheerful cooperation in a series of experiments. In one set of trials, conducted in Crookes's laboratory, the scientist assembled an ingenious weighing apparatus for the purpose of measuring Home's "power, force, or influence, proceeding from his hand." The physicist claimed to have recorded a pressure that was "equivalent to a direct pull of about 5,000 grains," or slightly less than three-quarters of a pound.

Try as he might, Crookes was never able to find an explanation consistent with the known laws of physics to explain Home's effects. He finally concluded that Home had mastered a new form of energy, "in some unknown manner connected to the human organization which for convenience can be called the Psychic Force." Crookes went on to suggest that in witnessing Home's force, the observer was inevitably put "in infinitesimal and inexplicable contact with a plane of existence not his own."

Perhaps even more puzzling than D. D. Home in reported powers of the paranormal was Eusapia Palladino. Born in southern Italy in 1854 and orphaned at the age of twelve, Palladino, too, allegedly became the center of spontaneous psychokinetic events as a young child. But it was not until the girl's late teens, when she came under the tutelage of a psychic investigator named Damiani, that the full extent of her alleged powers began to manifest itself.

Precisely what Damiani taught his rustic, uneducated, and rather indelicately mannered subject may never be known. But one thing seems clear—if Palladino truly had psychic gifts, she did not regard them as a precious trust. Whenever she sensed that she could get away with simple fraud, she was only too eager to take the easy route. And when caught cheating, the medium was quick to blame the nonbelievers in the audience who, she claimed, willed her to play tricks; in her trancelike state, she explained, she was incapable of defending herself against such dishonest suggestions. Nevertheless, occasions abounded when Palladino's paranormal effects—by one count she could call up thirty-nine different phenomena—seemed to defy all reason, however jaundiced the observer's view of her character might be.

In time Palladino came to the attention of Dr. Cesare Lombroso, a prominent Italian psychiatrist and criminal anthropologist with an avowed skepticism toward the paranormal. Lombroso went to Naples in 1890 to observe the young woman in action and, to his great surprise, came away a convert. Based on Lombroso's

Spiritualism's best-known physical medium, D. D. Home, intrigued the rich and the royal for more than twenty years with his mysterious séance effects.

favorable report, an international team of scientists and intellectuals invited Palladino to display her talents before them in Milan. The Milan Commission, as they were known, supervised a series of seventeen séances in 1892, and although Palladino seems to have had less than her usual success in the presence of these hoary heads, she was able to confound them with several partial materializations. According to the participants, she somehow had caused disembodied hands to float around the room and to touch the observers.

At the completion of their study the savants of the commission declared, ''It is impossible to count the number of times that a hand appeared and was touched by one of us. Suffice it to say that doubt was no longer possible. It was indeed a living, human hand which we saw and touched, while at the same time the bust and arms of the medium remained visible and her hands were held by those on either side of her.'' (These manifestations reportedly occurred even when Palladino's hands were tied to the chair in which she sat.)

It would appear that the only mildly dissenting voice among the commissioners was that of Charles Richet, professor of physiology at the Sorbonne, in Paris. ''It seems to me,'' Richet later wrote, ''very difficult to attribute the phenomena produced to deception, conscious or unconscious, or to a series of deceptions. Nevertheless, conclusive and indisputable proof that there was no fraud on Eusapia's part, or illusion on our part, is wanting: we must therefore renew our efforts to obtain such proof.''

No less an authority than Dr. Julien Ochorowicz, director of the Institut Général Psychologique in Paris, studied Palladino from November 1893 to January 1894. Ochorowicz ruled out the theory that spirits were behind the medium's alleged effects, concluding instead that the phenomena were the the work of Palladino's ''fluidic double.'' Taking Count Agénor de Gasparin's concept of ''psychic fluid'' one step further, Ochorowicz proposed that Palladino could summon up from this fluid a type of psychic twin that could, under certain circumstances, detach itself from the medium and act independently.

Colleagues from as far away as London and St. Petersburg, Russia, also took up Richet's challenge, and Eusapia Palladino found herself shuttling all over Europe to be examined further. But Richet, who would earn the Nobel Prize for Physiology and Medicine in 1913, was the most thor-

Under the watchful gaze of psychologist and psychic investigator Julien Ochorowicz,
Polish-born medium Stanislawa Tomczyk ostensibly causes a pair of scissors to float in midair
in 1913. Since the medium's hands were examined and washed before each séance,
Ochorowicz speculated that psychic "rays" emanating from Tomczyk's fingers guided the object's movement.

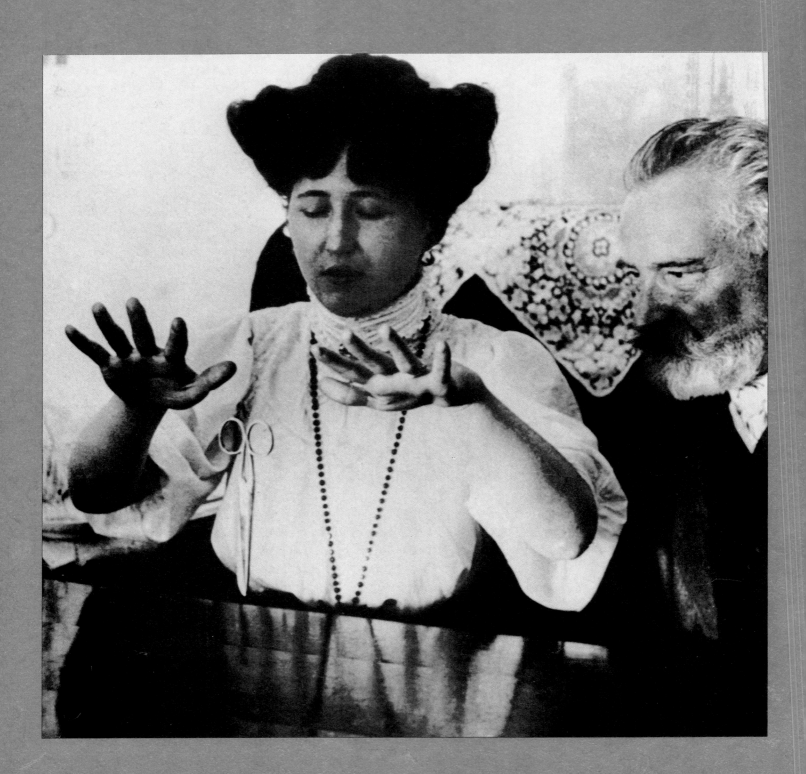

ough of the researchers. In 1894, he invited the peripatetic medium to join him on the Ile Roubaud, his private island off the coast of France; there, he reasoned, any possibility of accomplices or fraudulent devices could be removed. As an additional precaution, Richet invited two well-known psychical investigators, Frederic W. H. Myers and Sir Oliver Lodge, early members of the British Society for Psychical Research. Organized in 1882 by an eminent group of scholars in and around Cambridge University, the society's mandate was "to investigate that large body of debatable phenomena designated by such terms as mesmeric, psychical and spiritualistic."

As table tilting featured prominently in Palladino's psychokinetic effects, Richet had a sturdy table specially made for her. "The legs were pointed so that it would be difficult to raise it with the foot. . . . We thought . . . it much too heavy (forty-four pounds), but we tried it the same evening. As soon as Eusapia touched this heavy table with the tips of her fingers, it tilted, swaying about, and without the legs being touched at all, it rose up completely with all four feet off the ground."

After a series of séances, Richet and his British colleagues pronounced Palladino's powers genuine, and the SPR representatives invited her to Cambridge to perform before a full meeting of their organization. At the gathering, however, Palladino was caught cheating by one of her hosts, who had deliberately sought to entrap her, and she was sent packing in disgrace.

Back on the Continent, though, the more pragmatic European investigators, who acknowledged that the medium would always take shortcuts if given the chance, denounced the SPR and resumed their own investigations. One French researcher, M. Arthur Lévy, was thoroughly persuaded of Palladino's telekinetic skills after viewing a particularly unruly séance in which "the sofa came forward when she looked at it, then recoiled before her breath; all the instruments were thrown pell-mell upon the table; the tambourine rose almost to the height of the ceiling; the cushions took part in the sport, overturning everything on the table." One observer, Lévy noted, "was thrown from his chair. This chair—a heavy dining-room chair of black walnut—rose into the air, came up on the table with a great clatter, then was pushed off."

Before the séances, Palladino was usually undressed by female attendants and examined for any hidden implements that would aid in trickery. By the turn of the century, however, researchers were also using rather sophisticated electrical devices to evaluate psychic phenomena. And as reputable physicists at several of Europe's leading universities continued to record positive results from investigations of Palladino, the SPR decided to take another look.

In 1908, the organization sent three of its best—and most skeptical—investigators, including one who was a practiced conjurer, to meet Palladino in Naples. The British delegation produced a 263-page report detailing eleven separate séances and confessed that they had seen 470 events for which they could uncover no earthly explanation. One of the experts, F. H. Everard Feilding, concluded that "for the first time I have the absolute conviction that our observation is not mistaken. I realise as an appreciable fact of life that from an empty curtain I have seen hands and heads come forth, and that behind the empty curtain I have been seized by living fingers, the existence and position of the nails of which were perceptible. I have seen this extraordinary woman, sitting outside the curtain, held hand and foot, visible to myself, by my colleagues, immobile, except for the occasional straining of a limb while some entity within the curtain has over and over pressed my hand in a position clearly beyond her reach."

But Palladino's flush of success paled within a year; on a subsequent tour of the United States, she was caught cheating once again, and the effectively discredited medium all but disappeared from the séance scene. Nevertheless, in the minds of many investigators, an intriguing question still remained unanswered: How, they wondered, short of having genuine psychokinetic powers, did Palladino manage to achieve her many extraordinary feats without having

Dr. Alexander's Cloud-Busting Show

Knowing that their very survival can depend on the capricious ways of the weather, human beings have long sought to control the elements. Witches, shamans, and Druid priests, among others, have been credited with influencing the forces of nature—and in the view of some, such age-old powers continue into the twentieth century.

In 1956, for example, a sixty-five-year-old London physician named Rolf Alexander claimed he could dispel clouds by focusing upon them "a new kind of energy by which the human mind can act at a distance." Later that year, his alleged psychokinetic skills were put to a public test when he arranged a cloud-breaking demonstration for members of the press.

Skeptical journalists gathered with Alexander at Holne Tor, Devon, and watched as he began concentrating on a target cloud. Recorded in a timed series of photographs, the cloud disappeared in about four minutes *(left).* One baffled reporter later concluded that he found it "difficult not to believe . . . that Dr. Alexander can disintegrate clouds."

In fact, a review of Alexander's claims by Dr. Richard Scorer of London's Imperial College of Science and Technology revealed no evidence of cloud-controlling abilities. Indeed, Alexander conceded that his powers worked only on cumulus clouds—their equilibrium was so delicate, he claimed, that mind energy could readily neutralize their electrical charges. But Scorer and others schooled in meteorology knew that cumulus clouds normally change, disappear, and re-form within about fifteen to twenty minutes. In this case of alleged PK, Scorer concluded, the credit for cumulus cloud busting belonged to Mother Nature.

In his 1956 cloud-control display in Devon, England, Dr. Rolf Alexander concentrates on the three-cloud group visible at the center of the first photograph in the series at left. His object was to maintain the position of the two smaller clouds while dispelling the third, larger mass. The series of images, taken at thirty-second intervals, shows that in about four minutes, the two small clouds increased slightly in size, while the third one disappeared.

some of Europe's most skilled investigators detect fraud?

Skeptics, of course, would respond that even the most well-meaning scientists can be ill-equipped to see through the wiles of a talented conjurer, particularly if the investigators are predisposed to believe in the existence of paranormal phenomena. Fortunately for the world of parapsychology, Eusapia Palladino's checkered career only whetted the appetite of psi sleuths, and when Stanislawa Tomczyk's peculiar talents were discovered, researchers mounted renewed efforts to document psychokinetic prowess. The Polish-born Tomczyk was initially investigated in 1908 by Dr. Ochorowicz. Her association with spectacular poltergeist-like disturbances had gained her a certain notoriety in Warsaw, but these paranormal effects appeared to occur spontaneously and were beyond her control. What interested Ochorowicz more was that Tomczyk was able to produce those effects to order only while under hypnosis, when she seemed to assume the personality of a being she had named Little Stasia.

Little Stasia's special gift was levitating small objects. Typically, she would place her hands on either side of an object and about six to eight inches from it; she would then raise the object and move it freely in full view of her audience, who sat in a brightly lit room. Over a period of weeks, Ochorowicz observed a bell "feverishly shaken," a compass needle deflected, a "large pendulum . . . stopped mediumistically; then set going," and a host of other small objects rise and float within a bell jar, all of the effects apparently occurring as a result of Little Stasia's willing them to do so.

On one memorable occasion Tomczyk even unsettled Ochorowicz's spaniel. The dog, the doctor reported, was in the habit of lying quietly on the floor "near to an armchair about five yards from the couch, where the greater number of experiments took place. At the moment when the medium declared that Little Stasia had come and seated herself in the armchair, the spaniel, who was lying facing the chair, growled. I turned round and saw the dog's gaze fixed on the armchair. . . . He . . . repeated his growl three times. He only calmed down when the medium declared that Little Stasia was no longer there."

In an effort to isolate the force behind Tomczyk's levitational effects, Ochorowicz positioned himself at an extremely close range during her feats. He reportedly discovered that something rather like fine threads could be seen radiating from the medium's palms and fingers toward the objects being raised and manipulated. "I have felt this thread on my hand, on my face, on my hair," the investigator reported. "When the medium separates her hands the thread gets thinner and disappears; it gives the same sensation as a spider's web. If it is cut with scissors its continuity is immediately restored. It seems to be formed of points; it can be photographed and it is then seen to be much thinner than an ordinary thread. It starts from the fingers. Needless to remark that the hands of the medium were very carefully examined before every experiment."

Over the next few years, Tomczyk's psychokinetic feats were studied by a number of other researchers, including the SPR's Feilding, whom she married in 1919.

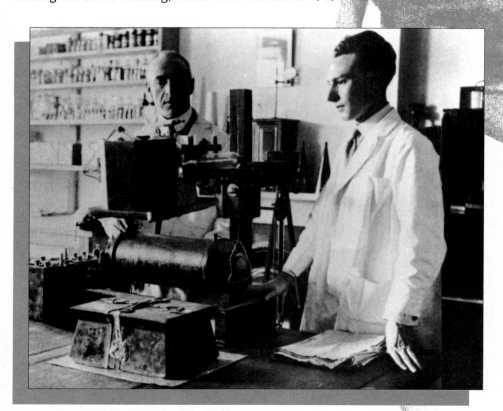

Psi researcher Harry Price (above, left), working with an assistant in 1927 in his London laboratory, was a student of the paranormal for more than forty years. He mounted his first investigation, involving a case of suspected poltergeist activity, when he was only fifteen.

Tomczyk never became a professional medium, however, and after her marriage she apparently declined to contact Little Stasia again.

Despite the earnest efforts of the SPR and its American counterpart—the ASPR, founded in 1885—to throw some light on the mysteries of levitation, table tilting, spirit rappings, and materializations, by the beginning of World War I most formal scientists had once again turned their backs on physical mediumship and psychokinesis. The discovery of numerous frauds among the self-proclaimed sensitives bred a mistrust difficult to overcome, and many who valued their reputations were reluctant to court the ridicule that was often heaped on serious students of PK. Then, in the 1920s, along came two discoveries that were sufficiently provocative to revive a lively interest in all quarters.

At the center of all the excitement was a rather flamboyant figure named Harry Price, the self-styled founder, director, and sole proprietor of the National Laboratory of Psychical Research in London. Price was by all accounts a

kind of puckish gadfly within the field of psychic studies. He had none of the formal training or academic titles so generously represented at the SPR and was a consummate self-promoter. But Price had certain advantages over his more learned colleagues—he was a skilled magician, adept at detecting fraud, and he was not particularly burdened with scientific methods of investigation.

It was only by chance that Price, making his daily train commute between London and his country home near Pulborough, met Stella Cranshaw. The two happened to strike up a conversation about matters psychic, during which Cranshaw, a rather modest young hospital nurse, told the investigator that she had been experiencing some very unsettling phenomena for several years—everything from odd rapping noises and "cold breezes" to household objects inexplicably taking flight. Price, excited by the prospect of a new research subject, identified himself as a specialist in the paranormal and invited her to his laboratory for testing; she reluctantly agreed.

Price was also an inventor and immediately set about

For his 1923 study of Stella Cranshaw (left), a young woman reportedly given to formidable displays of psychokinesis, Harry Price devised what he called a tele-kinetoscope, consisting of two bell jars fixed to metal bases. When a telegraph key sealed inside the larger jar was depressed—presumably by psychic means—a light inside the other jar would signal the investigator.

Harry Price (right) and research subject Rudi Schneider demonstrate specially wired socks and gloves designed to prevent fraud during séances. Any break in contact was signaled on a lighted indicator board.

designing an array of experimental equipment that he hoped would authenticate the young woman's claims. He built a special table for the séances; in addition, he placed thermometers around the séance room in his laboratory, each near a camera so that temperature changes could be recorded periodically. Most ingenious of all, however, was his "telekinetoscope," a clever device consisting of a telegraph key that, when depressed, completed an electrical circuit and caused a red light to flash. The key was both surrounded by an impermanent soap-and-glycerine bubble and covered by a bell jar; according to Price, only psychic energy directed toward the key could activate the device without disturbing the protective glass jar and breaking the delicate bubble.

During thirteen séances conducted between March and October of 1923—and always in the presence of several witnesses—Cranshaw went into ever-deeper trances as she ran through a spectacular repertoire of psychokinesis. On the third meeting, for example, Price reported that she managed to levitate the table so high that some of the observers at the séance were forced to rise out of their chairs in order to keep their hands on the tabletop. Then, the researcher continued, two of the table's three legs broke away "with a percussion-like noise" as the fracture occurred. But still more feats were to come. "Suddenly, and without warning, the tabletop snapped violently into two parts, and, simultaneously, the remaining leg and other supports of the table *crumpled up,* the whole being reduced to little more than matchwood. The sitting then concluded."

Price kept meticulous records of the gatherings and noted in his journal the temperature fluctuations during each séance—a drop of more than twenty degrees on one occasion—and the fact that Cranshaw had managed to ac-

tivate his telekinetoscope. But she was usually exhausted by the end of each session and eventually called a halt to the proceedings, claiming that the séances were causing her emotional as well as physical distress. Evidence uncovered after Price's death in 1948 suggests foul play, however: It appears that the investigator may have paid the young woman to abet him in an elaborate scheme to promote psychic research and, of course, himself.

Though Cranshaw's career as a medium was short-lived, her investigator's apparently careful handling of the case earned him the measure of prestige and respectability that he desired. Price, however, did not fare nearly so well with other subjects, notably the Austrian mediums Willi and Rudi Schneider.

The two brothers were initially discovered and trained by the respected German physician and psychical researcher Baron Albert von Schrenck-Notzing, who attributed to them remarkable feats of the paranormal. Price and SPR researcher Eric Dingwall were sufficiently intrigued to go see the brothers for themselves. Willi lived up to the advance billing, Price reported, displaying "many telekinetic movements." The British investigators took a variety of precautions against trickery—they arranged to have the young medium physically restrained by two other witnesses and, to avoid any manipulations with legs or toes, persuaded the boy to slip into "black tights, which were outlined with luminous bands and buttons." According to Price, "It was a wonderful display of phenomena, produced in really excellent red light."

But Willi's talents were apparently on the wane. Invited to England to perform before the SPR in 1924, he produced little in the way of psychokinetic effects and was roundly criticized by the group. Willi subsequently traded the psychic circuit for the more conventional life of a dentist. Not losing a beat, Price became interested in Willi's younger brother Rudi, whose psychokinetic gifts reportedly surpassed those of his older sibling. In 1929 Rudi traveled to Price's laboratory for tests that the investigator claimed, with some justice, represented significant advances in scientific verification techniques. Among many new wrinkles, Price wired the hands and feet of Rudi and everyone else seated around the séance table to a display board. A light would signal if and when anyone moved enough to break the electrical circuit.

Despite this control, Rudi was seen to produce a variety of psychokinetic effects, including ectoplasmic masses, rappings, and table tilting. Lord Charles Hope, a leading member of the Society for Psychical Research, was among the startled observers. At the end of this session, Price presented Rudi with a certificate on behalf of the laboratory, asserting that *"absolutely genuine* phenomena have been produced through his mediumship, under triple control conditions. . . . Not the slightest suspicious action was witnessed by any controller or any sitter."

The young Austrian next accepted an invitation to visit Dr. Eugène Osty and his son Marcel at the Institut Métapsychique in Paris. Osty's system for detecting fraud was even more ingenious than Price's. He positioned Rudi at a table and placed an assortment of objects in front of him. The doctor then focused an infrared beam in such a way that if Rudi's hands moved to touch the objects, the beam would be interrupted; a camera rigged to the device would then photograph him in the act of manipulation. What Osty did not anticipate was that something other than hands might also interrupt the beam. Over the course of the experiments and coincident with a series of intentional PK events provoked by Rudi, the beam's path was repeatedly broken. But when the resulting photographs were inspected, it was clear that Rudi's hands, held tightly by the investigator and his son, had not moved.

Osty theorized that the mental energy emanating from Rudi was enough to interrupt the beam, but he wanted to be sure. He then wired a bell to the infrared apparatus, repeated the experiments, and found that Rudi's ostensibly psychic emanations were of sufficient power and duration to ring the bell for more than sixty seconds.

Wishing to record and study the wave patterns of the beam at the moment it was impeded, the ever-thorough Osty introduced an oscilloscope to the proceedings. The resulting transcript showed that the oscillations produced on the infrared beam were consistently double that of Rudi's respiratory rate during the periods of alleged PK activity. For Osty, this was positive evidence of a direct connection between the PK phenomena and the medium's corporeal being. Students of the paranormal on both sides of the Atlantic found Osty's work admirable in its methods and compelling in its results.

Price must have felt a certain professional jealousy as the interest generated by Osty's work eclipsed that of his own earlier experiments. Price's goal was now to take photographs of Rudi's materializations, and in the spring of 1932, he called the young man back to London for more séances. Although Price obtained some favorable results, the sittings were not as successful as before—Rudi's talents seemed to be diminishing with age. In the fall, though, Lord Charles Hope conducted his own examination of the young man, and while he discovered that the results were indeed somewhat weaker than they had been in earlier tests, his findings generally supported Osty's.

And then, even as Hope was completing his report, Price lobbed a bombshell that rocked the psychical community. Rudi, he announced, was a fraud. As evidence, he produced a rather shadowy photograph purporting to show precisely the tricks the medium used to dupe everyone.

The immediate effect of Price's disclosure was to sully Schneider's reputation and to embarrass those researchers who had attested to his PK powers, including Price himself. As for Hope, he huffed that "neither the evidence Mr. Price adduces nor his method of presentation is such as to make his charges count for anything against a medium with Rudi's record. What does emerge damaged from Mr. Price's

This controversial photograph, taken at a 1932 séance organized by Harry Price, allegedly shows medium Rudi Schneider (seated, center) reaching for an object on a table. The camera had been set to record any movement by the medium, and while the resulting image was a double exposure and the action indistinct, Rudi's reputation as a medium was forever tarnished.

report is his own reputation as controller, conductor of investigations and critic.''

Indeed, allegations eventually surfaced that Price had tampered with the evidence in order to get revenge against his better-favored competitors, and though Price continued to study psychokinetic phenomena, his findings were often regarded somewhat suspiciously. But it was not until well after his death that the rumors about his deception were confirmed when the negative in question, which had apparently been doctored, was found among his personal papers. In many eyes, this discovery vindicated Rudi Schneider and restored him to the small ranks of presumably genuine psychokinetic talents.

By the time of Schneider's downfall, the appearance of credible new physical mediums had all but ceased. The Spiritualist movement, which had given birth to the mediumistic phenomenon and constituted its golden age, was itself in decline. The public had become jaded with séances that were frequently nothing more than amateur theatricals, and even the most unwavering researchers had begun to have serious doubts as to whether physical PK had ever been more than a mass delusion. Was it a coincidence, they wondered, that as new technology was making it increasingly possible to exert controls over the mediums, the mediums were disappearing? There were no takers, for example, when the SPR offered a £250 award to anyone who could produce PK under the eye of the society's infrared telescope, which enabled investigators to observe a medium's movements in the dark. Thus, scientific attention turned almost totally to matters of extrasensory perception and related forms of mental psi, which seemed to yield far more readily to attempts at replication and statistical measurement. Consequently, if there were worthy successors to the likes of Home, Palladino, Schneider, and the rest, they went largely unnoticed.

Then, more than three decades later, a new crop of PK practitioners began to emerge. But they were not mediums; these men and women did not confine their talents to the

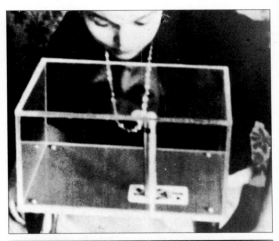

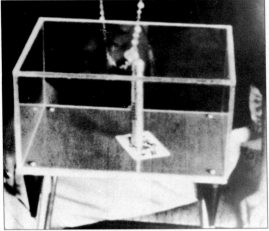

shadows of the séance room but displayed them in the unforgiving light of laboratories all over the world. One of the most important of this new generation was a Leningrad housewife named Nina Kulagina. Kulagina—also known as Nelya Mikhailova—first came to the attention of Leonid L. Vasiliev in the early 1960s, while Vasiliev was testing volunteers for "dermo-optic vision," the purported ESP ability to sense specific colors through the fingertips. Vasiliev, the Soviet Union's leading figure in parapsychology at the time, reported that when Kulagina was concentrating intensely, small objects on the table would sometimes move on their own when she placed her hands over them. This discovery led to extended studies of Kulagina's presumed psi powers, which were found to range from the original "eyeless sight" to the ability to deflect compass needles and levitate small objects.

Her brain waves monitored through an electrode-studded headpiece,
Soviet psychic Nina Kulagina focuses on moving an object inside a glass jar
during a 1960s test (above). She also seemed to scoot a playing card
and a cigar holder across the bottom of a sealed plastic box (center and top).

Sitters wait at an early 1850s séance conducted by Count Agénor de Gasparin, who studied group-produced PK.

Collective Psychokinesis

Since the Spiritualist movement began, some students of psychokinesis have considered that such supposedly paranormal effects do not always spring from the spirit world. One of the first to investigate alternate explanations for PK was French politician Count Agénor de Gasparin. After testing sitter groups in Switzerland, de Gasparin concluded in 1854 that telekinetic effects witnessed at séances were caused not by spirits but by those seated at the table. He believed that by communicating unconsciously, humans could influence an object with their collective will.

For some, this theory was confirmed in the mid-1960s, when members of Missouri's Society for Research on Rapport and Telekinesis (SORRAT) began holding weekly séances. The sitters displayed a lighthearted attitude, and the seeming PK effects—rappings and levitations—were often strong.

The animated approach successful for SORRAT was adopted by a similar Canadian group in 1973, but only after much trial and error. Eight members of the Toronto Society for Psychical Research had decided to conjure up a fictional spirit to test if group sightings of ghosts resulted from a col-

Iris Owen led the "Philip group" and co-wrote a book about the case; her husband, George, a parapsychologist, consulted.

lective hallucination. The group created a fictional seventeenth-century Englishman named Philip, who was married but also in love with a gypsy girl. When his wife learned of Philip's infidelity, she accused the girl of witchcraft and had

her put to death. Philip did not intervene and eventually killed himself in agony and remorse.

The Toronto group gathered weekly to discuss Philip and meditate in hopes of conjuring up his ghost. After a year without results, the group's leader, Iris Owen, suggested a different approach. She had seen a report by British researcher Kenneth J. Batcheldor, whose PK studies showed that a relaxed, jolly atmosphere encouraged paranormal phenomena. By lightly engaging the conscious mind, he claimed, one freed the unconscious to join the mental energies of others to produce PK.

Soon after adopting those techniques the group experienced table levitation and other PK effects and began to communicate with Philip through raps; as Iris Owen and group member Margaret Sparrow wrote in their 1976 book, *Conjuring Up Philip,* "it was like having a ninth person . . . joining in the conversation." Yet the sitters never forgot that Philip was imaginary. "We clearly understand and have proved that there is no 'spirit' behind the communications," Owen said. "It is the physical force we need to know more about."

A table tilts precariously beneath the hands of sitters gathered to summon the spirit of the fictional Philip.

With Vasiliev's death in 1966, other scientists took on Kulagina's case. Zdenek Rejdak, a Czech psychical researcher, filmed several controlled tests conducted with Kulagina in 1968. Rejdak reported—although the film did not confirm it—that Kulagina was first searched and x-rayed for concealed

Margaret Geller, here with Uri at age two, says she first noticed her son's metal-twisting talent two years later, when a spoon bent in his hand.

magnets or other devices that might affect results. Then, in full light and with several skilled observers seated around a table, she produced a series of effects using small objects, provided by Rejdak, that she had neither seen nor touched before the tests had begun.

One particularly impressive display involved a collection of wooden matches that were placed before her by the scientist. "We asked her to make the matches move not only toward her but also away from her," Rejdak explained. "We also asked her to move only one match, specified by us, from the whole group of matches." These PK effects, and many others, Kulagina completed to the observers' satisfaction. Rejdak concluded, "It appears therefore that the exteriorized energy can be directed by the subject's will."

Other investigators gradually developed a fuller description of Kulagina's supposed psychokinetic powers, finding that she could equally affect objects of metal, plastic, wood, and fabric; that when working with new materials she could move them away from her with ease, but toward her only with practice; that shielding objects with paper, acrylic, lead-impregnated glass, or even metal had no discernible effect on her performance; and that the greater the distance an object lay from her, the more energy was apparently required to move it.

Researchers also noted that when objects began to move, the direction paralleled Kulagina's own body movements. As she gained psychic control over the objects, however, they moved more freely in the requested manner. It was also reported that sparks sometimes emanated from her hands during PK and that her influence lingered on in the motion of target objects even after she had ceased will-

ing them, as though some residual energy in the object had to be exhausted. About the only limitation anyone discovered in Kulagina's powers was that she could not move objects that had been placed in a vacuum.

Not surprisingly, when the provocative articles and films of Kulagina's activities began circulating in the West, every psi researcher wanted to witness this marvel firsthand. Beginning in 1968, many succeeded, though under conditions that were often complicated by the rigors of the Soviet Union's closed society. Although the government barred full-scale controlled experiments of Kulagina, it permitted informal, impromptu demonstrations, either at her apartment or at the visitor's hotel.

All but a handful of the investigators came away convinced that they had witnessed genuine PK. Benson Herbert, a British parapsychologist, even claimed to have had the marks on his skin to prove it. He described having been gripped on his left forearm by Kulagina: "For two minutes, I felt nothing whatever, save only a natural increase of warmth under her hands. Then, quite abruptly, I experienced a new sensation . . . akin to a mild electric shock." After about two minutes, he reported, "I could not endure the sensation a moment longer, and disengaged my arm." For eight days thereafter, according to Herbert, he had a burnlike mark where the woman's hand had rested.

True to form, the critics—particularly in the United States—have dismissed Kulagina as a charlatan, maintaining that she manages her feats of alleged PK through the use of gossamer threads and cleverly concealed magnets. And while it is doubtful that the controversy will ever be settled to the satisfaction of all, Kulagina's supporters were considerably cheered in early 1988 when the Moscow newspaper *Pravda* reported the outcome of a legal action brought by Kulagina against a publication that had accused her of trickery. Two members of the Soviet Academy of Sciences testified on the plaintiff's behalf, swearing that her powers did not involve deception. The court ruled in Kulagina's favor and ordered the offending journal, *Man and Law,* to publish a retraction.

Whatever the truth about Nina Kulagina, the revival of scientific interest in PK led other alleged masters of mind control to step forward. Notable among them were two women, Felicia Parise of the United States and Alla Vinogradova of the Soviet Union; both reportedly developed a gift for PK after viewing films of Kulagina in action and were said to test successfully under laboratory controls. Another American studied in the lab, Ingo Swann, was reportedly able to influence ambient temperature and alter magnetic fields *(pages 74-75).* But of the new breed of psychics entering the PK limelight, none to date can match the performance—or the international fame and financial success—of the engaging young Israeli named Uri Geller.

When Geller, an individual of apparently wide-ranging talents and great personal magnetism, emerged in the early 1970s, he seemed for a time like a parapsychologist's wish come true. In his first two years of appearances in the West, Geller is said to have cooperated in more controlled experiments, undergone more sophisticated electronic monitoring, and baffled more psychologists and physicists than any other subject in the entire history of parapsychology. He toured virtually every continent, making appearances on scores of television, radio, and stage shows, thereby exposing members of the

general public to possibilities they had scarcely imagined before. But Geller's high visibility also had its negative side. No sooner was everyone talking about the "psychic boy wonder" than a host of critics committed to attacking him and debunking the "myth of PK" stepped forward to discredit him and pick holes in his claims.

Geller was born December 20, 1946, in the city of Tel Aviv, in what was then British-administered Palestine. His parents were Hungarian Jews; his mother was reportedly a distant cousin of Sigmund Freud, his father the grandson of an orthodox rabbi.

He was just three years old when paranormal phenomena allegedly began to happen in his presence, and in his 1975 autobiography, *My Story,* Geller suggests as a possible source of his powers "a strange energy force . . . a silvery mass of light" that he said had visited him one day when he was playing alone. At the age of four, a soup spoon ostensibly bent and broke in his hand, and by the

Members of the audience offer showman-psychic Uri Geller their stopped watches and clocks to restart during his tour of Israel in the mid-1980s.

time he was six years old, the boy had developed a reputation within the family for minor telepathic and precognitive skills—he supposedly knew before his mother came in the door the precise scores of her evening card games and how much money she had won or lost.

Geller spent his adolescence in Nicosia, Cyprus, but returned to Israel at the age of seventeen to serve in the armed forces. Trained as a paratrooper, he fought in the Six-Day War of 1967 and was wounded and subsequently discharged from the military. Up to this point, says Geller, he had made a conscious decision to keep his paranormal gifts pretty much to himself, as they were more likely to be regarded as mischief than miracle. Now, however, he took a job as a camp counselor and tried using them to entertain the children. He so fascinated and impressed his young charges with shows of telepathy and metal bending that one youngster, fourteen-year-old Shipi Shtrang, arranged to have Geller publicly demonstrate his psychic powers in 1969, at the boy's school in Tel Aviv.

One school performance led to many, and soon Geller was getting a great deal of newspaper publicity as well as offers from local theatrical agents and nightclubs. The handsome young mentalist with the intense eyes and winning smile—and no particular career goals—could hardly believe his good fortune. He left his job with a textile firm, signed with a professional manager, and became an overnight celebrity in his own country.

Controversy surrounded Geller from the beginning. The October 20, 1970, issue of the popular tabloid *Haolam Hazeh* ran a cover story under a banner boldly declaring Geller a cheat and followed up with an article that described why "all of Israel's magicians have assembled for a witch-hunt," with Geller as the prey. Part of the problem undoubtedly was professional jealousy; Geller the Psychic was a hard act to follow. But stage magicians also recognize a bit of trick-ery when they see it, and they may have been reacting to a particular segment of Geller's act. Allegedly at the insistence of his manager, he had begun to pad his show with a standard magician's trick: A confederate positioned in the parking lot outside the auditorium would write down a few license plate numbers from the cars of arriving customers, then deliver the innocent parties to selected seats in the theater. Geller, who had meanwhile memorized the numbers, would pick the drivers out of the crowd, seemingly at random, and call out their license plate numbers, leaving them and everyone else in the hall dumbfounded. Geller eventually admitted this instance of fraud but swore that it was the only time he had resorted to such trickery. He was, he said, young and foolish then and easily swayed by the advice of other people.

Meanwhile, Geller's dissatisfaction with his manager was growing week by week, and he wanted to break the contract. Geller also claims that he was interested to see how useful his psychic powers might be to science—and perhaps he expected that scientific validation would convince the magicians and his other critics to take him seriously. Then, in August 1971, Geller got all he wished for with the arrival of Dr. Andrija Puharich, an American physician with impeccable credentials in medical research and a reputation as a somewhat credulous investigator of paranormal matters. (Puharich claimed at times to be in touch with "space beings," and he had undergone psychic surgery, which its practitioners claim to perform without benefit of incisions.)

Puharich, who had heard about Geller from an Israeli colleague working in Boston, ran Geller through enough tests to convince himself that the young man possessed an extraordinary gift. The doctor then contacted several sponsors in the United States, including former astronaut and psi enthusiast Edgar D. Mitchell, and arranged to bring Geller to

For the first of many tests of his alleged psychokinetic powers, Uri Geller joined psi researchers Russell Targ (above) and Harold Puthoff at California's Stanford Research Institute in 1972.

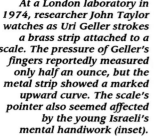

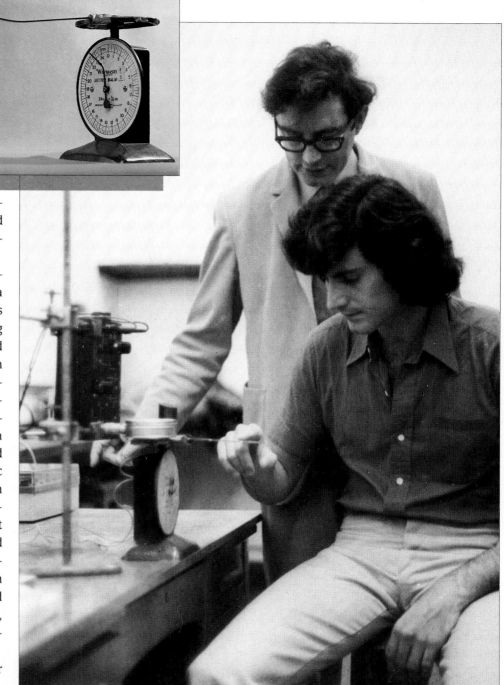

At a London laboratory in 1974, researcher John Taylor watches as Uri Geller strokes a brass strip attached to a scale. The pressure of Geller's fingers reportedly measured only half an ounce, but the metal strip showed a marked upward curve. The scale's pointer also seemed affected by the young Israeli's mental handiwork (inset).

California for further study at the Stanford Research Institute (later renamed SRI International) in Menlo Park, in order to assess his psi abilities.

During an initial visit with Mitchell in August 1972, Geller dazzled a number of scientists and researchers with informal displays of PK. During lunch breaks he bent their spoons and teleported tiny objects to their table. On one occasion, Gerald Feinberg, an esteemed physicist from Columbia University, witnessed an impressive demonstration. Geller asked a woman present to take off her gold ring and hold it in her closed fist; the psychic then waved his hand over hers. When the woman uncurled her fingers, according to Feinberg, the ring at first "appeared with a crack in it, as if it had been cut through with a very sharp instrument." Geller then laid the ring on the table, Feinberg continued, and "over the period of a couple of hours, the ring twisted so that it went gradually into the shape of an 'S.'"

The following November, Geller went to California to begin formal testing with physicists Harold Puthoff and Russell Targ at SRI. The two researchers were most interested in Geller's alleged telepathic and clairvoyant abilities, and their research agenda included thirteen different experiments in "information transmission." For most of the testing, Geller was locked in a double-walled steel room, shielded visually, acoustically, and electrically from the outside world. His task was to "see" target pictures selected at random—grapes, a firecracker, a rabbit, a church—by scientists in another room and to reproduce the images as precisely as he could with paper and pen.

Geller's success rate was reportedly high—in the case of the grapes, he even sketched the correct number of grapes in the bunch. He was also asked to guess the uppermost face of a die, randomly cast inside a steel box, in a series of ten double-blind trials. On the eight occasions when Geller answered, he responded correctly; he chose to pass the two other times, claiming he had received no clear mental impression of the die. Targ and Puthoff concluded that the odds for Geller's success based on chance alone were about a million to one.

The SRI investigators compiled their results in a formal paper and submitted it to one of the most prestigious scientific publications in the West, the British journal *Nature.* After some professional soul-searching, described in a leading editorial, the journal broke precedent and published the article in October 1974. While the editors felt there were shortcomings in the methodology of the experiments, they expressed the opinion that Targ and Puthoff had dealt with "phenomena which, while highly implausible to many scientists, would nevertheless seem to be worthy of investigation even if, in the final analysis, negative findings are revealed." The journal's editorial also noted that "contrary to very widespread rumour, the paper does not present any evidence whatsoever for Geller's alleged abilities to bend metal rods by stroking them, influence magnets at a distance, make watches stop or start by some psychokinetic force, and so on."

SRI was not interested in testing Geller's psychokinetic abilities, but other scientists were, and Geller moved on to work in their laboratories. One of the most interesting studies was conducted in 1973 and again in 1974 by Eldon

Byrd, a scientist at the Naval Surface Weapons Center in Silver Spring, Maryland. An avid student of the paranormal, Byrd was intrigued by tales of Geller's metal bending and wanted to see how the young Israeli would fare with nitinol, a remarkable new metal alloy developed by one of the center's metallurgists. Nitinol's distinguishing characteristic is its "memory." The material can be bent, crumpled, creased, and twisted beyond recognition—but with exposure to heat, it returns to its original manufactured shape. Byrd, who undertook his work with Geller on his own, without any government sponsorship, theorized that if the young Israeli truly interacted with metal in some psychokinetic way, then he might be able to erase that memory.

Byrd handed Geller a five-inch length of nitinol wire. His subject looked at it briefly and then asked Byrd to hold the wire taut at both ends while he stroked it. After about twenty seconds, Geller said he felt a lump forming in the wire and stopped rubbing it. When Geller lifted his fingers, Byrd saw a U-shaped kink in the center of the wire. As the investigator recalled later, "This particular wire was

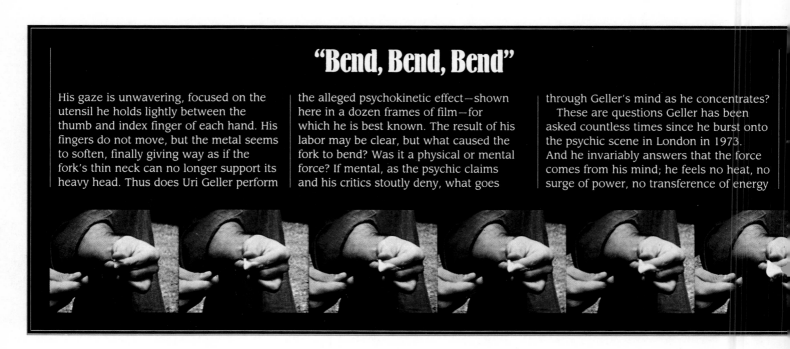

"Bend, Bend, Bend"

His gaze is unwavering, focused on the utensil he holds lightly between the thumb and index finger of each hand. His fingers do not move, but the metal seems to soften, finally giving way as if the fork's thin neck can no longer support its heavy head. Thus does Uri Geller perform

the alleged psychokinetic effect—shown here in a dozen frames of film—for which he is best known. The result of his labor may be clear, but what caused the fork to bend? Was it a physical or mental force? If mental, as the psychic claims and his critics stoutly deny, what goes

through Geller's mind as he concentrates? These are questions Geller has been asked countless times since he burst onto the psychic scene in London in 1973. And he invariably answers that the force comes from his mind; he feels no heat, no surge of power, no transference of energy formed, at the time of manufacture, in a straight configuration, and immersion in boiling water should have caused it to spring back vigorously to that shape. *But when I placed it in the water, the wire, instead of snapping back with some force into a straight shape, began to form approximately a right angle . . .* I lit a match and held it over the kink, but still the wire did not straighten out."

Although critics would later insist that Geller might have found some way to obtain and tamper with a length of nitinol before his session with the scientist, Byrd could not discover any logical explanation for the changes that had occurred in the wire sample. When he had a chance to meet with Geller again a year after the study, he arranged to repeat the experiment.

This time he had added some elegant refinements. The wire was checked for anomalies at Byrd's laboratory and was configured to return to a straight shape upon heating. Byrd cut a length of nitinol wire into four pieces, giving three to Geller and retaining the other as a control. Two of the lengths were held by Byrd as Geller stroked them, and the third was held by Geller; kinks appeared in all three samples. When Byrd heated the wires to the temperature that normally would invoke their memory, the kinks remained as before. The deformed pieces were then analyzed by x-ray crystallography, a scanning electron microscope, and other precision instruments, but the results offered no clues as to how Geller had apparently changed the metal alloy's physical properties.

Summing up his findings, Byrd asserted, "I can say that the possibility of fraud on Geller's part can be virtually ruled out. Because of the unusual properties of nitinol, the scientific controls essential for any investigation are, for the most part, built into the testing material. Geller would have had to 'palm' a source of high heat or substitute his own personally manufactured or previously altered pieces of nitinol if deception is to be the explanation for the events that took place—two highly unlikely possibilities."

Unlikely, but apparently not impossible, according to magazine columnist and amateur magician Martin Gardner—a member of the executive council of the militantly

to the object. He simply focuses, he says, and repeats to himself "bend, bend, bend." Geller suggested in a 1988 interview that all people may have "some kind of kinetic energy that comes from our minds or brains, something which can't be measured." He says he possesses an abundance of this energy, which is channeled from his mind to the object he focuses on. While Geller is a religious

man and views his talent as a special gift from God, he does not discount the possibility that he may have tapped into a type of "extraterrestrial power."

Whatever the source of his professed mental energies, Geller maintains they are stored until such time as he depletes them with PK efforts. "I use up nearly all of them every time I bend something," he wrote in 1986, "it takes at least half

an hour for me to refill my energy pool." Geller admits he sometimes fails to perform a PK feat. While such failures are embarrassing, for him they are also a kind of vindication. "If I were a professional magician," he explains, "I am certain I would practice to the point where I, like they, would never fail. As it is, I would make a pretty miserable excuse for a professional magician."

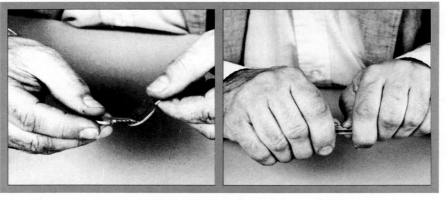

skeptical Committee for the Scientific Investigation of Claims of the Paranormal. Countering Byrd's assertion that nitinol was not generally available to the public, Gardner wrote in the May/June 1977 issue of *The Humanist,* a magazine frequently featuring articles debunking the paranormal, that the wire was available to magicians at the time of Byrd's experiments. Gardner, an ardent critic of Geller, further claimed to have permanently kinked a section of nitinol wire himself. Given his suspected skills as a conjurer, Gardner observed, Geller could easily enough have worked his apparent wonders through trickery.

Perhaps so, but Geller also received high marks in 1974 from William Cox, a research associate at

Magician James Randi (top) shows how Uri Geller might bend keys through quick sleight of hand after momentarily distracting observers: He could insert the tip of one key into the slotted head of another and exert pressure (above, left) or use a lightweight key or one that is deeply cut and bend it between his thumbs (above, right).

the widely respected Institute for Parapsychology in Durham, North Carolina, and himself a practiced magician. Cox arranged a meeting with Geller in New York at which he presented the psychic with several PK challenges, the most impressive of which involved Cox's own seventeen-jewel pocket watch and Geller's vaunted ability to restart broken timepieces. In preparation for the test, Cox inserted a piece of aluminum foil between the spokes of the balance wheel so that the watch could no longer run; he then placed another piece of foil over the watch's internal regulator arm and set the arm to the very limits of the "fast" position. Cox satisfied himself that no amount of shaking would dislodge the foil or start the watch and that the two hinged covers

protecting the works could not be pried open except with a small knife or jeweler's tool. He handed the timepiece to Geller, saying only that it would not run.

Geller examined the watch carefully—he held it to his ear, shook it gently—but always within Cox's full view; within thirty seconds the watch was ticking. When Cox opened the back of his timepiece to see what had happened, he found the regulator arm moved completely to the "slow" setting, which he estimated as being roughly forty degrees counterclockwise. The foil was cut in two and rested at a ninety degree angle from its original position.

Cox also tested Geller's celebrated metal-bending abilities. The research associate had brought with him an ungrooved steel safe-deposit-box key that measured just over two inches long. Geller laid the key upon the surface of a glass coffee table and asked Cox to press lightly on the key's broad handle; under Cox's watchful eye, Geller stroked the key's other end. In less than a minute, Cox reported, the key had bent to an angle of about twelve and one-fourth degrees.

Were this to have been done by normal means, the investigator declared, it would have taken an upward force of nearly forty pounds at Geller's end or about one hundred pounds downward at Cox's, neither of which was possible under existing conditions. Cox pronounced the metal-bending skill "novel in the history of psi phenomena" and urged his fellow magicians and psychical researchers to investigate Geller's gifts further.

One who took Cox's advice was John Hasted, professor of experimental physics and head of the physics department at Birkbeck College, University of London. Hasted had been among the viewers when Geller made his first television appearance in England in 1973 and was intrigued by the young man's feats. Early in 1974, Hasted invited Geller to Birkbeck to meet with him and other physicists on the faculty. Over the next few months, Hasted—who described himself as skeptical of paranormal phenomena in general but capable of observing dispassionately—became increasingly perplexed by what he and his colleagues saw.

During one session, Hasted handed Geller a stainless steel spoon that already had allegedly been bent paranormally by a previous research subject. According to Hasted, "Geller held the handle and did not touch the bend. Within a few seconds, and under our close scrutiny, the bend in the spoon became plastic. It quickly softened so much that the spoon could be held with one end in either hand and gently moved to and fro. I had never seen Geller produce a really plastic bend before, and I asked him to hand the spoon to me in one piece. . . . It was as though the bent part of the spoon was as soft as chewing gum, and yet its appearance was normal."

At another session, Hasted placed his hand between a plastic capsule, containing a thin shaving from a type of brittle crystal, and Geller's hand, which was hovering about eight inches above the object. Wrote the astonished Hasted, "I swear I felt a warm sensation, as though I were experiencing strong diathermic heating." A moment later, he reported, the capsule gave a little jump as if suffused with energy; when the physicists examined the capsule's contents, they found that half of the crystal shaving had unaccountably vanished.

The Birkbeck team also watched Geller send a Geiger counter into convulsions, with readings soaring as high as 500 times the normal rate of background radiation, merely by holding it in his hands. He also reportedly caused a compass needle to deflect from its normal magnetic alignment and break loose from its bearings.

The Birkbeck researchers noted—as did many other investigators—that unlike most psychics, Geller did not experience any shifts in consciousness when performing psychokinetic feats. As a result, they theorized, he was highly sensitive to the attitudes of those testing him. When the observers seemed to be feeling tension, hostility, fear, or other negative emotions, Geller tended to perform poorly or not at all. By contrast, when the atmosphere of the meeting was very positive, he seemed to be especially energized, as though drawing some of his power from those around him. (Geller has said as much in describing the source of his PK powers: "I have never been able to bend or break an object unless there are at least one or two other people in the room.") The Birkbeck group came to the conclusion that Geller's performance improved when he found the tests challenging and surmised that rigid conditions normally desirable in scientific experimentation hindered him in bringing forth the kinds of surprising and unpredictable results that he was otherwise capable of.

Uri Geller's key-bending method seems simple: He sets the key on a table and strokes it. Some say the key continues to contort even after he stops rubbing it, thus ruling out fraud.

Critics assert that the relaxed conditions that seem so conducive to Geller's PK effects would also allow him to resort to sleight of hand or other trickery without detection. Those who subscribe to this belief include science writer and astrophysicist Carl Sagan, science-fiction writer Isaac Asimov, and a number of other members of the Committee for the Scientific Investigation of Claims of the Paranormal, a group that includes both magicians and respected American scientists. But surely the most committed of Geller's many critics is James "The Amazing" Randi, a professional stage conjurer who, like Harry Houdini of an earlier generation, has taken a special interest in exposing the practitioners of "psychical" fraud.

Randi first observed Geller face to face in the Manhattan offices of *Time* magazine in 1973. Geller and Puharich, his sponsor, had come to demonstrate the young man's powers to a skeptical editorial staff preparing to do a feature on Geller and the SRI findings. Randi had heard of the impending meeting and arranged to pose as a *Time* reporter—Geller's "allergy" to magicians being well known. With his practiced eye, Randi watched the performance intently, appearing to be as intrigued as anyone while Geller went through his basic repertoire of metal-bending and telepathic feats. But after Geller and Puharich had left, Randi proceeded to produce all the same effects, using techniques familiar to any skilled stage magician.

Unhappily, from Randi's point of view, his instant "exposure" of Geller and *Time*'s subsequent panning of the psychic did not turn back the tide of enthusiasm that seemed to grow exponentially as the public became familiar with Geller's activities. Suddenly, apparently as a result of Geller's international television appearances, hundreds of "mini-Gellers" surfaced in his wake. Scores of these self-confessed cutlery crimpers, the majority of them children, were tested by investigators who were able to confirm, to their own satisfaction at least, that a significant number seemed to exhibit genuine psychokinetic powers.

One Geller clone who appeared to out-warp even the master of metal bending was Silvio Meyer, a young Swiss who first came to public attention in 1974. Meyer not only bent spoons readily but was reported to have broken them in two, then "psi-soldered" the pieces without so much as touching them. To show Meyer's PK at work, one such spoon was thus restored with the shank of the spoon reattached so that its underside faced up; it now resides in the archives of the Freiburg Institute.

While psychical investigators such as Birkbeck College's John Hasted wrestled with the questions raised by the appearance of the Geller disciples, Randi made it his sworn mission to unmask the Israeli Wonder once and for all. The uncompromising magician was proud of his profession and resented what he scornfully referred to as Geller's "prostitution of the art."

Since then, Randi has dogged Geller's heels, reproducing many of the mentalist's most widely publicized psi phenomena through conjuring tricks demonstrated openly. On one occasion, Randi secretly coached television personality Johnny Carson and his staff on how to prepare for a Geller appearance on the "Tonight Show." He suggested that the keys and spoons Geller would require be purchased new and that all props, including any broken watches for Geller to "repair," be kept under lock and key before the broadcast. Furthermore, Randi instructed the members of Carson's staff not to allow Geller or any of his entourage to see or touch the props until the actual demonstration was to begin. Perhaps as a result of such rigid controls, Geller was unable to give a single demonstration of psychokinetic powers that night. Geller, however, blamed his lack of success on nerves and the time constraints that had been imposed by the show's producers.

In 1975, with his dossier on Geller presumably complete, Randi published a lengthy, combative book entitled *The Magic of Uri Geller* (later republished as *The Truth about Uri Geller*), intended to expose the "naivete of learned men in all parts of the world." In its more than 200 pages, Randi gives step-by-step descriptions of how keys may be bent by sleight of hand *(page 32)* and stopped timepieces restarted

by such normal, earthly means as "accidentally" jarring them or by palming them for a few moments in order to warm thickened oil. He describes at length what he regards as the sloppy experimental controls that had been imposed on Geller. And he ridicules everyone from SRI researchers Puthoff ("an adherent of . . . a nut religion") and Targ ("very nearsighted") to the Birkbeck College physicists ("the English will believe anything"). Andrija Puharich comes off even worse in the book, as someone whose mind is clouded by hallucinogenic drugs, and Geller is described as positively dangerous, a self-styled "semi-religious figure with divine pretensions . . . the false Messiah."

Randi's unrestrained attack probably did play a part in dimming Geller's star. Controlled laboratory investigations of the engaging young Israeli all but stopped in 1975, though whether it was because Geller had in fact become an outcast within the scientific community is difficult to determine. And, certainly, Randi's book outlines a strong case for including professional magicians in the design of future experiments in psychokinesis, regardless of who the subject of investigation might be.

But as Geller explained it, he was simply tired of being at the center of "Gellermania." The role of scientific guinea pig was physically as well as emotionally exhausting, and the financial rewards were scant compared with what he thought awaited him as a PK pop star and business consultant. Moreover, it occurred to Geller that the continuing controversy—was he psychic or showman?—had greater value than would his being understood by scientists. "Publicity, whether it's negative or positive, is always good publicity," he has said. "It keeps my name out there somewhere." In 1976, Geller went off to seek his fortune in earnest. And in this pursuit, too, he appears to have succeeded as no psychic before him.

At first Geller toured the capitals of the world as a stage and television performer, traveling with an entourage that has been compared with that of rock music stars and royal potentates. In addition to Shipi Shtrang, his friend and sometime manager since 1969, he was often accompanied by Shipi's sister Hanna and an assortment of personal secretaries and press agents. Geller also became a star of the social circuit. Handsome, charming, confident, and by some accounts a "hypnotic personality," he regularly turned up at presidential inaugurations and attended state dinners from Mexico City to Geneva and Tokyo, chatting genially with the likes of Jimmy Carter, Henry Kissinger, José López Portillo, and Sophia Loren.

Not surprisingly, he also came to the attention of some imaginative corporate leaders, who wondered if Geller could harness his talents in some ways useful to them. As one mining magnate reportedly observed, "There's more money in finding metal than bending metal."

Eventually, even the jet-set life proved to be tiring, and in 1979, at the age of thirty-three, Geller married Hanna Shtrang. He and his wife now live rather privately with their two children on a grand country estate outside of London. He currently heads a consulting company called Uri Geller Associates, which markets his supposed psi skills as a means of locating significant deposits of metal ores, coal, and petroleum. With the help of geologists who select areas that seem to be generally favorable, Geller scans a region first from maps; then, from an airplane, he tries to sense ore deposits; finally, he walks the area, hands extended, as though finger dowsing. He makes his recommendations reportedly on the basis of "an inner feeling . . . some kind of pressure in my hands . . . intuition."

Geller also has laid plans to offer his forecasting services to the financial community and claims to consult occasionally both on major criminal investigations and on government intelligence work. He has written four books to date, including the novel *Pampini,* about a psychic superman who is caught up in the Cold War.

For a fee, he has allowed marketers to use his name and trademark symbol, the bent spoon, on toys and games, jewelry, clothing, health foods, and natural cosmetics. And he continues to perform before live audiences and on television from time to time, just "to keep my name out there somewhere." All told, in a span of ten years he claims to have earned around a hundred million dollars from his many enterprises.

As if all this were not enough, Geller reportedly gets called upon occasionally for some high-level consultations. He claims to have been in on some secret psi work with a major international medical laboratory, putting his psychic energies to work on cancer cells and strains of the AIDS virus. And in the spring of 1987, he was by some reports a United States diplomat-without-portfolio at the Geneva arms reduction talks.

Though verifiable details are scanty, Geller claims his assignment was to mingle with members of the Soviet delegation at an American reception and dinner, "eavesdrop" mentally on their negotiating intentions, and beam back some positive "peace thoughts" on behalf of the United States. When the newspapers got wind of Geller's presence, the chief American negotiator was quick to explain that Geller had been invited only as an entertainer—but the psychic seemed not at all surprised to learn the following day that the head of the Soviet delegation had just returned to the bargaining table with a new and unexpectedly generous disarmament proposal.

Such cloak-and-dagger stuff appalls the legions of Geller's critics, who have worked almost as diligently to expose him as a mountebank as Geller has to gain celebrity. And yet, as his supporters never tire of pointing out, Geller has never been indisputably proven a fraud. True enough, he may have cheated in inducing some of his psi effects, he may be distressingly temperamental and egotistical in his dealings with investigators, he may shun all observers whom he knows to be hostile to his work and perform poorly or not at all in the company of people he "senses" are antagonistic to his claims. But such behavior, Geller's supporters say, does not in itself rule out the possibility that Geller is also capable, under favorable circumstances, of producing genuine ESP and PK effects. It only makes full and final evaluation more difficult—which may, indeed, be exactly what Uri Geller wants.

The World of Poltergeists

In 1851 the quiet village of Cideville, eighty miles northwest of Paris, was the site of a witch trial. Almost by definition, such events tend to be more than a trifle bizarre, but this one was even stranger than most. For the case was brought by the alleged witch, a shepherd named Felix Thorel, and the defendant was none other than the village priest, a Father Tinel.

The chain of events leading to this improbable case began the previous year, when Father Tinel paid a call on an ailing parishioner. The patient, the priest discovered, had been treated with the medicines of a local charlatan who claimed to be a practicing sorcerer. When the parishioner died soon afterward, Father Tinel had the so-called sorcerer arrested and thrown into jail. From his cell, the sorcerer vowed to take revenge.

The revenge, if such it was, took a strange and roundabout form. At the time, two young boys were living in Father Tinel's parsonage. One day at an auction in Cideville, the shepherd Thorel—who was a disciple of the jailed sorcerer—stopped the boys, placed his hands upon their heads, and murmured a mysterious incantation. In the months that followed, Cideville ceased to be a quiet village for the priest and his pupils.

According to the trial records, no sooner had the boys returned to their room in the parsonage than a fearsome gust of wind rocked the building. That night, a loud and persistent rapping noise disturbed their sleep; no cause could be found. Over the next two months, a series of increasingly freakish events transformed the once restful parsonage into a scene of nightmarish madness. Tables skittered across the floor, candlesticks and fireplace tongs danced in the air, and chairs and carpets hovered over the heads of astonished visitors.

By far the most unrelenting of the many reported disturbances was the loud rapping, which sounded as though someone were striking the wainscoting of the room with a hammer. In time, Father Tinel and the marquis de Mirville, a nobleman who had come from Paris to investigate the well-publicized incidents, initiated a crude form of communication through these rappings. The marquis was able to deduce that the entity that was wreaking havoc at the parsonage had a paralyzing fear of nails, spikes, and other sharp points.

Tables, chairs, and even a dog and cat sail above the heads of an astonished Father Tinel and his housekeeper at the parsonage in Cideville, France, in 1850.

Immediately, he and Father Tinel began driving nails into the floor and walls of the room wherever the strange manifestations had occurred. It is said that the first of the nails instantly glowed red-hot and that the floor crackled and smoked. When another nail was driven into a cupboard, Father Tinel's elder pupil reported a fleeting vision of a nail tearing a man's cheek. The following day that vision appeared in the flesh: The shepherd Thorel was seen with an ugly gash on his cheek that looked as though it had been made by the sharp point of a nail. As far as Father Tinel was concerned, that proved the man's guilt. He accused the shepherd of witchcraft and knocked him to the ground with his walking stick. Unexpectedly, Thorel responded by suing the clergyman for libel.

Thorel not only lost his suit, but he was compelled to pay court costs. Still, he had one victory. Father Tinel reluctantly agreed to let his pupils leave the parsonage. Only then was peace restored.

From Folklore to Freud

Although the events in Cideville were thought at the time to be witchcraft, in later years some students of the paranormal have suspected the presence of a poltergeist. The term poltergeist—from the German words *poltern,* meaning to make noise, and *Geist,* meaning ghost or spirit—describes a curious kind of allegedly psychic phenomenon characterized by strangely mischievous, almost teasing events that defy easy explanation.

If there was a poltergeist in the parsonage, it behaved true to form. Typically, when a poltergeist is said to be at hand, there are mysterious rappings and bangings and gusts of cold air. Objects move about inexplicably: Crockery tumbles to the floor and furniture flies through the air. Sometimes doors and windows fling open by themselves, items disappear only to be found in the next room, stones and rocks mysteriously bombard buildings, and in a few rare cases, people are physically attacked. Often, these events take place in the presence of a child or adolescent.

Over the centuries, countless broken windows and shattered plates have been blamed on these restless spirits. Undoubtedly most of the mishaps have had human causes. Indeed, many psychical researchers are reluctant to admit that the phenomenon exists at all. Skeptics point out that many so-called paranormal rappings and creakings could have far more mundane explanations, such as shrinking timbers or the effects of underground streams. Early in this century, no less an

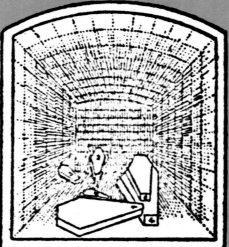

Contemporary sketches show the Chase family vault at the last burial there, in 1819 (top), and when it was reopened a year later (bottom). The movement of the coffins over the years was thought by some to be the work of a poltergeist.

authority than Frank Podmore of London's Society for Psychical Research advanced a "naughty little girl" theory, holding that many disturbances attributed to poltergeists owe less to the supernatural than to children's overheated imaginations and love for pranks.

Still, a number of modern psychical investigators take a more serious view of poltergeists. Researchers such as Hans Bender of West Germany and William G. Roll of the United States not only believe in poltergeists but reject the long-held notion that they are discarnate, or noncorporeal beings. The poltergeist, in their view, has little or no independent existence. Rather, it is a "person-centered" phenomenon, triggered within the subconscious of a living, human agent.

In many cases the presumed agent seems to be experiencing great personal unhappiness or frustration, which may, in some unknown fashion, be expressed as a powerful psychokinetic force. Some theorists have even suggested that the onset of puberty, with all its attendant anxieties, may trigger a poltergeist.

Although researchers still seek to understand the genesis of poltergeist activity, they have detected certain patterns over the years. Foremost of these is that the occurrences are never single, isolated incidents. Rather, the poltergeist tends to stretch out its visits over weeks and months, sometimes even a period of years. For this reason, many psychical researchers use the phrase "recurrent spontaneous psychokinesis" (RSPK) to describe poltergeist phenomena.

An Unquiet Grave

What was uncanny about the poltergeist that reportedly haunted a family tomb on the Caribbean island of Barbados, then, was not that it stayed for years but that it appeared to be location centered rather than person centered. Prominent landowners on Barbados in the early nineteenth century, the Chase family first became aware of something peculiar in 1812, following the death of their daughter, Dorcas. The Chases had a plain stone burial vault in a small church graveyard not far from Bridgetown. Scarcely had Dorcas's body been interred there on July 6 than the rumor sprang up that the young woman had starved herself to death in despair over her cruel treatment at the hands of her father, Thomas Chase, a man much hated on the island.

The rumor intensified a few weeks later when Thomas Chase himself died suddenly. This time, members of the funeral party found a bizarre scene when they opened the family vault. Dorcas's coffin had been tossed against the back wall of the tomb like so much driftwood. Two other coffins had been similarly flung about.

The callous treatment of their dead naturally angered and distressed the grieving Chase family. Grave robberies were not unknown on Barbados, but nothing appeared to have been taken from the vault. And a vandal would have had to chip away the cement that sealed the heavy marble slab at the entrance, hurl the coffins across the chamber, and then carefully seal the entrance again. As unlikely as this seemed, no one came forward with a more plausible explanation.

Three more burials followed within seven years. Each time the vault was opened, the coffins—including the massive, 240-pound one of Thomas Chase—were found wildly jumbled together, although the sealed door of the vault appeared undisturbed. And by the second of the three burials, the matter had become a source of such speculation that the governor, Lord Combermere, got involved.

Under Combermere's supervision, a team of men searched the vault, but before resealing it, they sprinkled sand on the floor so they could detect the footprints of any intruder. A few months later curiosity compelled Combermere and his men to return to the graveyard. The seal appeared as they had left it, and after hours of chipping away at the cement, they entered the chamber—only to find it more violently chaotic than before.

Some of the coffins leaned drunkenly against the walls. Others were strewn carelessly atop one another, and one had flipped over completely. Yet not a footprint marred the pristine smoothness of the sand on the floor. Combermere, admitting that the mystery was beyond him, ordered the coffins removed from the vault and buried in another location. Since then the vault has reportedly been untroubled.

There have been other accounts of moving coffins over the years, but in most cases the problem has been easily explained; sometimes they were shaken up by an earth tremor, sometimes carried by floodwaters that then receded and set them down in a different place. Neither of these explanations applied to the Barbados case. The Chase family vault never showed any sign of flooding, and a tremor capable of upending a 240-pound coffin would not have gone unnoticed by the living. In the absence of any natural cause, speculation quickly turned to the supernatural.

Many observers of the period, as well as others who subsequently reviewed the events, were struck by the fact that the disturbances began after the interment of young Dorcas Chase, the suspected suicide. Some students of the paranormal speculate that the violent movement within the vault was the result of her "restless spirit"—a poltergeist that hovered near her earthly remains.

If that is the case, the story of the moving coffins of Barbados represents one of the rare instances in which a reported poltergeist did not attach itself to the living. It would also be one of the few cases in psychic research in which a poltergeist has plagued a place rather than an individual; the disturbances tend to focus on a single, living person. And in the entire history of poltergeist phenomena, probably the most famous such person was Eleonora Zugun.

The Poisoned Candy

In the best fairy-tale tradition, the story of Eleonora begins with a little girl going to visit her grandmother. In February 1925 Eleonora, a twelve-year-old peasant living in the northern Rumanian village of Talpa, set out to see her grandmother, who lived in a village nearby. The girl found some money by the road and bought candy with her windfall. But when she told her grandmother of her lucky find, the old lady flew into a rage. The money had been left there by malicious spirits, she declared, and Eleonora, having eaten the candy, had absorbed the devil, too.

The devil, or whatever it was, reportedly made itself known the next day. In Eleonora's presence, small objects began to jump up and fly through the air; stones showered down on the grandmother's cottage,

Photographs taken in Harry Price's National Laboratory of Psychical Research show the results of alleged attacks on Eleonora Zugun in the 1920s. Welts on her face and bite marks on her hands and arms appeared as Price and his assistants observed.

shattering windows. When villagers learned of the strange happenings, Eleonora was sent home to Talpa. There, not three days later, the phenomena resumed with even greater violence.

In despair, Eleonora's parents took her to a priest to be exorcised of evil spirits. But far from being put to rest, the poltergeist proceeded to put on its most impressive show yet. Bystanders, includ-

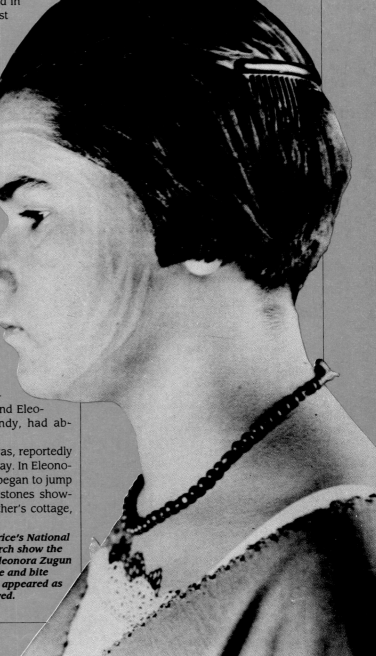

ing the stunned priest, watched in amazement as a water-filled jug sailed through the air without spilling a drop and a trunk began to rock. One observer even received a blow across the face from a flying kitchen cutting board. Eyewitnesses agreed that Eleonora could not physically have been responsible for such events.

Perhaps not, but as the poltergeist persisted, Eleonora was ostracized even by her parents. The girl found temporary refuge in a local monastery; when the violent activities continued even there, she was moved to a lunatic asylum. By then the case had been the subject of considerable newspaper coverage, and the publicity had attracted the attention of psychical investigators. Among them was a Viennese countess named Zo Wassilko-Serecki, who said she was convinced that Eleonora was the victim of a poltergeist. In January 1926 the countess removed the girl, by now dirty and frightened, from the asylum and brought her to live in Vienna.

For the first time since she had eaten the "tainted" candy, Eleonora appeared happy—but the phenomena grew even more horrible. Within two months of

moving in with the countess, Eleonora seemed to be under physical attack by an unseen tormenter. Scratches and welts appeared on her face, neck, and arms. On one occasion her hands and arms turned purple from as many as twenty-five apparent bites. In her diary, the countess wrote that she had seen the painful marks emerge "exactly as though [Eleonora] had been bitten by somebody," even as she held the girl's hands.

Harry Price, a noted British researcher who had come to Vienna to observe Eleonora, was equally impressed by the vivid bite and scratch marks and by such events as a seat cushion floating through the air. "Some of the telekinetic phenomena witnessed by me were not the work of normal forces," he stated. And that September, Price invited Eleonora and the countess to the National Laboratory of Psychical Research in London, then a leading force in the investigation of the spirit world.

For two weeks, Eleonora was subjected to every manner of psychic test available. Although much of the phenomena—notably the movement and disappearance of various objects—was less impressive than it had been in Vienna, Price managed to record a graphic series of photographs of the bites and scratches that kept appearing on the girl's face and hands.

While Price was convinced of their authenticity, others were dubious. The following year, when Eleonora and her patron were on a visit to Munich, a medical doctor accused the countess of inflicting the wounds on the girl, under the guise of tidying her hair or examining a scratch. The countess angrily denied the charges, noting that even if she had accidentally

The case of the Schrey family of West Germany in 1946 supposedly provided vivid photographic evidence of poltergeist activity. Shown from left to right, the evidence included a pen, an iron file, and a razor blade, all broken and twisted in ways that investigators were unable to duplicate; a heavy rug that appeared to tie itself in knots; Irma Schrey's hair, hacked off as if by an invisible blade; and mysterious messages composed on Carola Schrey's typewriter.

scratched the girl, she could not have bitten her without being detected.

Whatever the truth, the supposed poltergeist attacks stopped a few months later, when Eleonora began to menstruate for the first time. Then, after two years of fear and pain, Eleonora resumed a normal life in Rumania.

Eleonora Zugun's case proved to be a milestone in the study of poltergeists, ushering in a new era of research and prompting a reappraisal of a number of cases, with a greater emphasis on the human focus. Perhaps the most significant new theory advanced during this period was that of the British parapsychologist Hereward Carring-

ton, who was one of the first to discern a connection between human biology and reports of poltergeist activity. Writing in 1930, Carrington theorized that the onset of puberty in adolescents, together with additional, unknown factors, might bring on poltergeist phenomena. "An energy seems to be radiated from the body," the researcher speculated. "It would almost seem as if these energies instead of taking the normal course . . . find this curious means of externalization." Alan R. G. Owen, a British geneticist and mathematician with an abiding interest in the paranormal, later expanded on Carrington's thesis.

While pointing out that a number of poltergeist cases apparently center exclusively on adults, Owen acknowledged that many poltergeist agents have ranged in age from ten to twenty years old. "It is by no means clear," he wrote in 1970, "that the poltergeist disturbances coincide at all precisely with pubertal changes. However, there may be something to be said for a modified form of Carrington's theory in which we think not of physiological energy but of emotional tension which can occur both before and after puberty."

Luckily, not every adolescent going through puberty has a poltergeist. But the theory that emotional tension can act as a kind of trigger for poltergeist activity is borne out again and again in the records of psychical investigators. Certainly, emotions ran high in the case of Carola and Otto Schrey and their two daughters.

"Ditti Did It"
The Schreys' troubles had their roots in the upheaval of World War II. Having fled Allied bombardment in western Germany, the Schreys settled down in a small apartment in the Bavarian village of Lauter. During their relocation, they became foster parents to a thirteen-year-old girl named Irma, who had lost her real parents a few months earlier. Later the couple took in yet another orphan, a three-year-old named Edith. The Schreys eventually adopted Edith, a beautiful,

well-mannered little girl, but not Irma, who was frequently truculent and withdrawn.

In June of 1946, Edith, whose nickname was Ditti, underwent an alarming personality change. The once placid girl became unruly and even spiteful, and her constant tantrums terrorized the family. When confronted about her behavior, the child would say only, "Ditti did it because I am not allowed."

Though a rebellious child is hardly the stuff of the supernatural, Edith's black moods reportedly marked the beginning of months of horror. Soon the child sank regularly into trancelike states. During these periods, according to Carola Schrey, the household become a virtual sewer. Piles of human excrement and pools of urine materialized in every corner of the small apartment—under the furniture, on the kitchen floor, even in the beds. At first Carola Schrey assumed that one of her daughters was responsible and went so far as to withhold liquids from the girls. But the foul messes persisted.

Things continued to deteriorate for the Schreys. Irma began to fall into the same trancelike lethargy that plagued little Edith. Ink pens, iron files, and razor blades broke into fragments. Religious pictures were spattered with tomatoes; liverwurst flew out of the frying pan and into the cleaning supplies. Indecipherable messages were typed on Carola Schrey's portable typewriter, although the machine was securely locked in its carrying case.

The disorder turned to violence one day as Irma was carrying a box of firewood into the house. As the girl entered the kitchen, in full view of her foster parents, one of

In photographic reconstructions, Franz and Maria Plach gaze at lights symbolizing errant dinner rolls and laundry. Below, a moving bowl of soup disrupts dinner plans.

her long braids fell to the ground as if lopped off by an invisible blade. Later, the rest of her hair would be viciously hacked away, leaving her scalp bloody and raw. One cut penetrated the skull.

At this point, there appeared on the scene Hans Bender, the parapsychologist who was founder and director of Freiburg University's Institute for Border Areas of Psychology and Mental Hygiene. In previous investigations, Bender had found that his presence had a dampening effect on poltergeist activity, as though the noisy spirits shrank from scrutiny by outsiders.

But whatever entity was troubling the Schreys displayed no such reticence, according to Bender. He was interviewing the Schrey couple during one of his first visits to their apartment when the presumed poltergeist announced itself in no uncertain terms. Moments after Irma came into the room, closing the door behind her, the adults heard loud noises coming from the hallway. Throwing open the door, they found that a heavy rug stored there had been twisted so wildly that it took all three of them several minutes to straighten it out.

Bender came away convinced that the Schreys were the victims of a genuine poltergeist—and he thought he knew the source. Although both Schrey girls had been caught up in the disturbances, Irma, the adolescent, seemed the likelier focus. That she, unlike Edith, had not been officially adopted by the Schreys might have been a source of resentment—or "emotional tension," as Alan Owen would call it. And that, in turn, reasoned Bender, may have triggered the poltergeist's unwelcome visit.

Like all such hauntings, the disturbances at the Schreys' home diminished over time and eventually ceased altogether. But even as the Schreys' lives returned to normal, a similar nightmare reportedly began for the Plach family, only a few miles away in the mountain village of Vachendorf.

The Flying Wooden Shoe

On March 16, 1947, Maria and Franz Plach were playing cards in their living room with their fourteen-year-old adopted daughter, Mitzi. As the game went on, all the players found that they were holding fewer and fewer cards. When some of the missing cards reappeared under the table, the Plachs naturally assumed that someone had dropped them there and dismissed the incident. But when they dealt a new hand, the cards vanished once again. And this time, they did not resurface. By the end of the evening there were just nineteen cards remaining from the fifty-two-card deck.

Forced to abandon their game, the Plachs shrugged and went to bed—only to confront a greater mystery. Because the Plachs' home was small, Mitzi slept in the same room with her parents. That night,

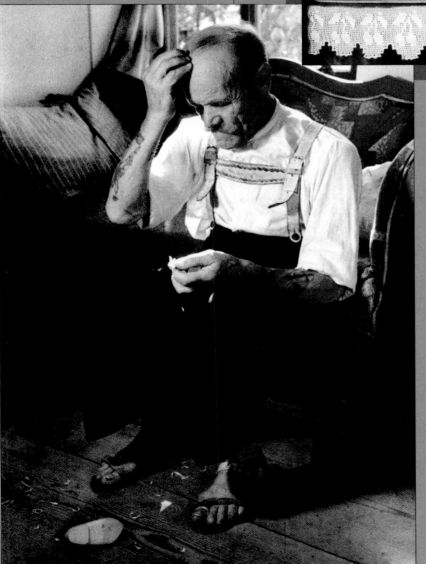

however, no one slept. No sooner had the lights been turned off than the Plachs found themselves pelted by a hailstorm of hammers, knives, coal, water, stones, and dirt. Shielding his face with his hands, Franz Plach leaped out of bed to turn on the light, but the bulbs had somehow been loosened in their sockets. When the family attempted to flee from the bedroom, they discovered the door was locked. Later, after neighbors had broken down the door and released the terrified family, the missing key was spotted hanging from a clock in another room.

Unfortunately for the Plachs, the night of the flying objects was only a prelude to days of continuing aerial mischief. Laundry left hanging in the attic would float and cavort about the house. Dishes would come sailing out of a cupboard and crash against the opposite wall, falling unbroken to the floor. A bowl of soup skated along the table and emptied its contents into Franz Plach's lap. Rolls that Mitzi had brought home flew about the kitchen like "so many swallows," Maria Plach wrote in her diary, while the butter moved incautiously toward the oven and melted.

The Plachs fought back, but to little avail. When Maria gathered up all the loose objects in the house, put them in a box, and locked the box in a closet, the items simply flew out again, apparently penetrating both box and locked door. The next day, the same sequence occurred. "It was no use," Maria wrote. "I grabbed everything, put it into the box and sat on it, but it all came out again."

Once again Hans Bender arrived on the scene, this time bringing along a photographer, Leif Geiges, in hopes of capturing the strange manifestations on film. Failing that, Bender reasoned, it might be useful to re-create some of the events to provide a visual record of the case. The Plach family's mysterious visitor avoided portraiture, as it turned out, but it proved to be far from shy.

In fact, one of the more baffling and violent episodes took place in the presence of the intruding investigator. As Franz Plach

Franz Plach rubs his forehead as he studies the wooden shoe that struck him. The shoe had been stored in a glass cabinet (inset), on top of a drinking mug that, ironically, appears to share the secret.

worked absorbedly on a wood carving, a heavy wooden shoe flew across the room and struck him in the head with a resounding smack. Bender's photographer caught the somewhat rueful expression on the victim's face seconds after the blow. When Plach recovered, he pointed out that the shoe had been kept in a glassed-in cabinet that was still intact. The bizarre incident, according to the researcher, was "a clear case of telekinesis and a case of matter penetrating matter."

Just as Bender had zeroed in on the sullen Irma Schrey, this time his attention was drawn to teenaged Mitzi Plach. When Bender learned that the poltergeist activity had ceased while Mitzi made a brief trip away from home, his suspicions were confirmed. Once again, a girl in the early stages of puberty appeared to be the focus of a poltergeist visitation. Although the sources of emotional tension were not quite as obvious in the Plach family, the parallels to the Schrey case seemed to be clear. Happily the Plachs' apparent haunting, like the Schreys', soon stopped as abruptly as it had begun.

Though Geiges's photographs helped dramatize the nature of an alleged poltergeist experience, Bender remained frustrated in his attempts to record an actual poltergeist at work. But investigators in the case of Teresa Costa were more fortunate.

A Saucepan on the Wing
In 1955 Costa, a young Italian woman, was visiting friends in the small town of St. Jean de Maurienne in the French Alps when the friends' home suddenly came alive with phantom rappings and flying kitchen utensils. Three policemen summoned to the scene bore witness to the strange goings-on.

Costa fell into a trance and was hospitalized overnight. No sooner had she been released, however, than washboards and kitchen stools took to the air. A photographer snapped a picture just as a saucepan sailed past the frightened woman.

In the absence of the meticulous Bender, the Costa case was never thoroughly re-

searched, and the admittedly blurry photograph is hardly conclusive evidence. But the fact that a snapshot exists at all underscores one of the most frustrating aspects of the phenomenon. Poltergeist activity is, by its very nature, a teasingly evasive, corner-of-the-eye affair that eludes the grasp of the most assiduous investigator or subject. People visited by poltergeists often report glimpsing a shadowy movement that disappears as soon as they confront it head-on. In fact, a number of investigators have even theorized that the

Teresa Costa shields her infant son from a whirling saucepan and scissors during a stay in the French Alps in 1955. The photographer vows that the image is genuine.

human eye possesses a sort of checking mechanism that somehow stops the poltergeist in its tracks.

Unbottled Spirits in Seaford
A suspected poltergeist of Seaford, Long Island somehow managed to evade an army of police, psychical researchers, and press. The extraordinary chain of events began on February 3, 1958, in the three-bedroom home of James and Lucille Herrmann. At half past three that afternoon Lucille Herrmann was startled to hear a long series of popping noises, as though a doz-

en champagne bottles had been placed throughout the house and then suddenly uncorked. Calling to her two children—Lucille, aged thirteen, and James junior, aged twelve—she rushed to investigate.

If what she found had not been so bizarre, it would have been laughable. In virtually every room of the house, one or more bottles of various kinds had apparently opened spontaneously. In the Herrmanns' bedroom, a bottle of holy water was uncapped. In the bathroom, shampoo and medicine had spilled onto the floor. In the kitchen and basement were puddles of bleach and liquid starch. What made the matter all the more puzzling was that each of the bottles had been securely sealed with a screw-on cap, rather than a cork or bottle cap that might have popped off more easily. Nor had any of the bottles contained carbonated liquids that might have produced an explosive gas.

By the time James Herrmann returned from his New York City office that evening, his family had mopped up the various liquids. Though no one could explain what had happened, the Herrmanns agreed to forget the matter. That proved easier said than done.

Three days later, at roughly half past three again, six more bottles blew open and spilled their contents onto every floor of the house. The performance was repeated the following day and again two days later. After the fourth round of explosions, James Herrmann called the police. The seasoned police officer who responded was predictably skeptical—until his questions to the family were drowned out by the sound of still another series of exploding bottles.

Detective Joseph Tozzi, the resourceful and clearheaded police veteran assigned to the case, was convinced that there was a simple physical explanation for the explosions, and he set out to find it. Perhaps, the detective speculated, the bottles had been bombarded by high-frequency radio

The Herrmanns of Long Island examine a heavy bookcase that had mysteriously toppled. Many of their favorite possessions were systematically destroyed during several weeks in 1958.

transmissions. A ham radio operator lived nearby, but Tozzi learned that he had not used his transmitter for three years. A check with the air force eliminated the possibility that sonic booms had caused the explosions. An oscilloscope in the cellar failed to detect any unusual vibrations.

Meanwhile, bottles continued to pop, and other objects in the Herrmanns' home also seemed to be taking on exuberant lives of their own. Tozzi, along with members of the Herrmann family, reported seeing a porcelain figure float through the air and a sugar bowl hurl itself against the dining room wall. On another occasion, with all four family members gathered upstairs, a heavy bookcase crashed to the floor of the basement.

Within two weeks after the first bottle popped, the case had been widely reported by the press, and letters of support and advice began to pour in. One correspondent suggested that visitors from outer space had caused the trouble and cautioned the Herrmanns to be polite to them. Another blamed a Soviet satellite. Some suspected that a poltergeist was at work and that its focus was young Jimmy Herrmann.

Still others suggested that Jimmy might be perpetrating an impressive hoax on his family and the Nassau County police. The boy was bright and imaginative and had a known fondness for science fiction and other fantastic adventure stories. According to published accounts of the case, most of the disturbances had occurred when he was in the same room or nearby, and a few times—such as when a phonograph flew across his bedroom, an event that newspapers promptly dubbed "The Case of the Hi-Fly"—Jimmy had been the sole witness. It seemed possible, then, that the boy had staged the entire affair as an elaborate prank. But Tozzi, for all his eagerness to find an explanation for the strange happenings, thought otherwise.

So did two prominent parapsychologists who arrived at the Herrmanns' home in late February. J. Gaither Pratt and William G. Roll, associates of the noted Duke University researcher J. B. Rhine, refused to dismiss the matter as a mere prank, but from the first they focused on the Herrmanns' young son. Pratt, particularly, moved quickly to the conclusion that Jimmy had unconsciously sparked the events.

A great believer in the power of the mind to influence matter, Pratt once remarked, "It is within the realm of possibility that if eight million New Yorkers at one time concentrated on moving the Empire State Building, it might move a bit."

Hoping to witness a poltergeist manifestation firsthand, Pratt spent a great deal of time with Jimmy, but nothing out of the ordinary occurred. Nevertheless, he felt certain that what was taking place at the Herrmanns' was nothing less than recurrent spontaneous psychokinesis—in short, a poltergeist. His colleague, Roll, advanced the speculation another step. Under Hereward Carrington's theory of the troubled adolescent, either Jimmy or his sister Lucille might have been the agent. When lengthy conversations with Jimmy revealed an aggressive and frustrated personality lurking beneath the boy's placid exterior, Roll believed he had found his poltergeist focus.

An Easter Poltergeist

Like most alleged poltergeist hauntings, the Herrmanns' visitation was short lived, ending abruptly one month after it had begun. And like nearly all such events, the disturbances were relatively benign. But sometimes poltergeists are dangerous—especially when they involve fire. And for five consecutive Easters, that was precisely the threat that hung with alarming punctuality over Graham and Vera Stringer, a young English couple.

The first fire broke out in the Stringers' small London apartment during Easter week in 1958, after the couple and their baby son, Steven, had gone to bed. The flames destroyed a sackful of Steven's toys that had been left on a chair in the living room. The Stringers discovered and extinguished the flames before they could do more serious harm and counted themselves lucky.

On Good Friday of the following year, Vera Stringer returned from shopping to find her husband battling another fire in their living room. A carton of gifts from Vera Stringer's mother had burst into flame while Graham Stringer and Steven were in another room. Once again, the fire was brought quickly under control, though all the gifts were ruined. The next year, fire struck again. On the day after Easter, Vera

Stringer was in the kitchen when she smelled something burning. In the bedroom, a shirt and undershirt belonging to her husband were on fire, and a chest of drawers was badly scorched before the flames were put out.

By Easter 1961, the Stringers were braced for another fire. Indeed, their fire insurance had been canceled because of the mysterious regularity of their claims. But whatever was responsible for the blazes refused to be so boringly predictable. There were no fires that year. The Stringers did report that twice they saw a peculiar "grey column of fluorescent light" wafting through the apartment, accompanied by the phantom sounds of footsteps and of doors opening and closing. Later they found that a kitchen window had been smashed. Only partly tongue in cheek, the Stringers concluded that their small apartment had been invaded by a poltergeist and, having recovered their sense of humor in a fire-free Easter, they named it Larry.

For all their irreverence, the Stringers awaited the 1962 Easter season with trepidation—and rightfully so. That year brought the most serious fire yet. Flames shooting to a height of three feet greeted Vera Stringer in the living room one morning. The fire department soon controlled the blaze, but Larry had not finished. Later that day, even as the Stringers were cleaning up from the first blaze, a second fire broke out in their son's bedroom. Luckily, Steven was not in the room at the time, and there was no serious damage.

To the Stringers' relief, subsequent Easters passed without a visit from Larry. No one ever traced the purported poltergeist to a single human focus—it was impossible to say which family member, if any, might have been the agent—or otherwise explained the flames. One theory advanced by psychical researchers is that such seemingly spontaneous combustion may be the result of some sort of molecular agitation by the poltergeist. That is just a theory, of course. But the fire was real.

It Followed Her to School

While the Stringers were putting out fires in London, an eleven-year-old girl in the village of Sauchie in central Scotland was having a mysterious visitor of her own—

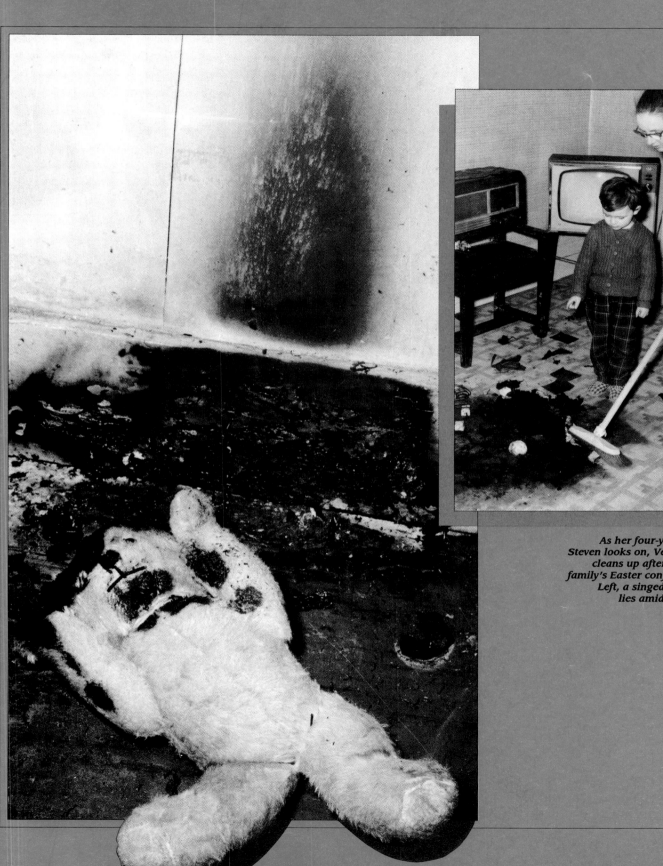

*As her four-year-old son
Steven looks on, Vera Stringer
cleans up after one of her
family's Easter conflagrations.
Left, a singed teddy bear
lies amid the debris.*

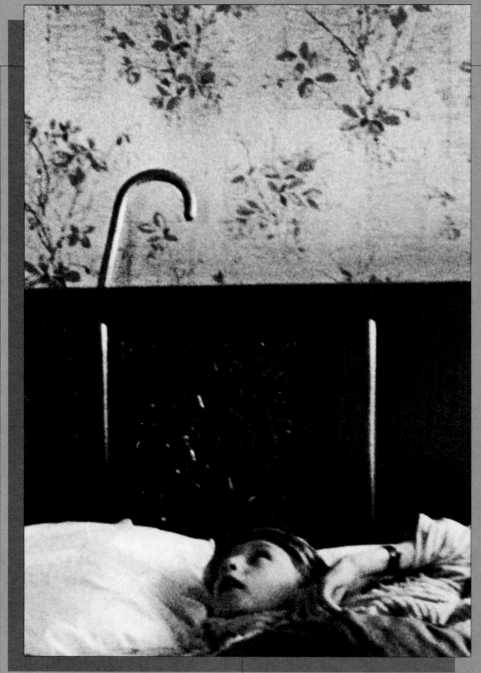

and, as in the nursery rhyme about Mary and her little lamb, it even followed her to school. The youngest daughter of an elderly farming couple in Ireland, Virginia Campbell was staying with her brother and his wife in Sauchie toward the end of 1960 while her parents were making preparations to settle in Scotland. Apart from being big for her age, Virginia was an unremarkable child—a bit shy but bright and fond of games.

That was before the evening of November 22, when Virginia came downstairs to complain that a "thunking" sound in her bedroom, like a bouncing ball, was keeping her awake. The next day her brother and sister-in-law reportedly saw a heavy sideboard move five inches; Virginia was sitting nearby but not touching it. Summoned by a neighbor of the Campbells, the local minister arrived at midnight to investigate; he heard inexplicable knocking and saw a large linen chest levitate. When he returned the next night, he watched the pillow beneath Virginia's head rotate sixty degrees. A physician who dropped by agreed that the pillow moved, that there were knocking sounds, and that the linen chest moved occasionally.

After a two-day absence, Virginia returned to school on Friday—but her supposed poltergeist seems to have tagged along. First the lid of Virginia's desk moved up and down. Then the empty desk behind the girl rose about an inch. On Monday, the alleged poltergeist became more playful. A blackboard pointer vibrated and edged off a desk onto the floor. The teacher's own desk rotated counterclockwise. Virginia, regarded with suspicion although her hands were clasped behind her back, burst into tears. "Please, Miss, I'm not trying it," she said.

That evening Virginia was sent to stay with an aunt in a neighboring town. It was hoped that the poltergeist would not follow her there, too, but the knocking sounds continued. They persisted—and were captured on a tape recorder—when Virginia returned to Sauchie. Soon, however, the disturbances subsided, with Virginia and her nine-year-old niece, Margaret, with whom she shared a double bed, reporting only an occasional pinch. In January the poltergeist returned to school, where it supposedly moved a bowl of flower bulbs. By March, though, it seemed to have departed, and Virginia, according to her teacher, had become less shy.

If there are such things as poltergeists, Virginia was certainly an appealing target: a girl who was going through puberty, with rapid physical development, and who was clearly anxious about the other changes in her life. During this time she also fell into trances in which she spoke about her life in Ireland and called out longingly for her dog and another little girl who had been her friend. There were indications, too, that Virginia was unhappy sharing a room with her niece—a sentiment underscored when the supposed poltergeist responded with loud and angry knocking to a suggestion that Margaret rejoin Virginia in bed. Skeptics might argue that Virginia, rather than a poltergeist, was rejecting the suggestion. But only Virginia could know for certain whether that was true.

The Dancing Cane

The case centering on a fourteen-year-old English boy named Michael Collindridge also had all the classic elements: an adolescent, a floating object, even a photograph. But ultimately, the poltergeist itself proved a bit shaky.

In November of 1965, Michael was confined to bed with tonsillitis at the apartment of his grandmother, Sarah Shepherd, a pubkeeper in the Yorkshire town of Barnsley. Hanging on the headboard of Michael's bed was a lightweight Malacca walking stick, which his grandmother had used while nursing a broken leg twelve years earlier. As Michael lay staring at the ceiling one day, he reported, the walking stick began to float above the headboard and bob up and down.

Soon the cane grew livelier, dancing around the room, dipping under the bed, and darting to the window. But it always came to rest on the headboard. Then Michael found that he could induce the cane to rap out the answers to simple questions— whether there would be a war within the next year, say—and tap out "Jingle Bells." It even posed for a newspaper photographer. Dozens of witnesses attested to the un-

canny movement of the cane, and all were baffled. "I got that stick twelve years ago from my sister-in-law," Sarah Shepherd reported. "It never performed any antics until Friday."

Under questioning, Michael readily admitted that he had long had an interest in magic, even putting on occasional performances for his friends. He insisted, however, that the dancing cane was not a trick. "I'm not very good at conjuring," he said with disarming candor. When pressed for an alternative explanation, the boy hypothesized that "it is something to do with centrifugal force working in conjunction with cosmic rays."

Newspaper reports of the cosmic cane piqued the interest of Andrew Mackenzie of London's Society for Psychical Research. Although the walking stick proved uncharacteristically immobile when Mackenzie was present, the investigator collected a number of persuasive eyewitness reports of its movements. A close examination of the stick turned up nothing suspicious, and Mackenzie left Yorkshire uncertain whether a poltergeist or a prankster was at work. "Short of taking a sick boy out of bed and stripping down his bed, I do not see what more could have been done," he said later.

But others suspected that even sick boys just want to have fun. The president of a British magicians' club denounced all the speculation about a poltergeist, noting that any reasonably talented magician can make a walking stick dance. Believers in the spirit world retorted that just because a magician can duplicate a supernatural phenomenon does not mean that the phenomenon itself is not supernatural. Soon Michael put an end to the debate: Recovered from his tonsillitis, he got out of his sickbed, and the cane settled down on the

Miami warehouse clerk Julio Vasquez, the alleged agent of hundreds of poltergeist manifestations, undergoes brain-wave tests in 1967.

headboard. Some twenty years later, however, he returned to the room and maintained his innocence.

Days and Nights of the Zombie Glasses

While the controversy that developed around Michael Collindridge involved the alleged movements of only a single object, the cane, a variety of items figured in a series of strange events in a warehouse in Miami, Florida, the following year. In December of 1966, Alvin Laubheim, a co-owner of a business dealing in novelty items and souvenirs, was becoming concerned over the high rate of breakage of beer mugs and other items in his company's warehouse. He told his two shipping clerks, Curt Hagemayer and Julio Vasquez, to be more careful. Painstakingly, he showed the clerks how to arrange the mugs in a row at the back of a shelf, eight inches from the front edge, with the handles turned to the wall to prevent their being jostled. Laubheim completed his lecture and was walking away when the familiar sound of breaking glass brought him to a halt. Even though all three men were at least fifteen feet from the shelf, one of the meticulously placed mugs had crashed to the floor.

Glass continued to break over the next few days, and the losses grew so serious that Laubheim telephoned the police for help. "This guy has got to be a nut," muttered the patrolman who had been assigned to investigate. But as the officer stepped into the warehouse he saw a solitary beer mug crash to the floor. A few hours later, three more policemen watched in fascination as a carton filled with address books inched to the edge of a shelf and tumbled off.

Many more novelty items plunged from Laubheim's storage shelves in the days that followed, including dozens of plastic back scratchers, several boxes of alligator-shaped ashtrays, and a number of so-called zombie glasses, highball glasses painted with palm trees and flamingos. A flock of newspaper reporters, professional magicians, and insurance investigators converged on the warehouse in order to observe the activity, but no one was able to explain it.

Once again, parapsychologists Roll and

Pratt, investigators of the Herrmann family poltergeist, came to the rescue. Methodically, they analyzed the data relating to 224 unexplained breakages in the warehouse. Although neither man actually saw any object levitate or fall, they were in the warehouse when several such incidents occurred and, by cordoning off certain areas and monitoring Laubheim and his employees, satisfied themselves that the disturbances were not being faked.

Their experiences in other cases led the two parapsychologists to zero in on Laubheim's younger clerk, the nineteen-year-old Vasquez, who had been present for most of the breakage. A Cuban refugee, Vasquez exhibited much of the suppressed frustration that Roll and Pratt had observed in young James Herrmann during the Seaford incident. In particular, Vasquez seemed to harbor a great deal of anger toward one of the warehouse bosses, but he had to stifle his rage because he wanted to keep his job. At one point he

Skewed paintings (above) and bills for multiple phone calls to the 0119 time-of-day number (below) were results of the strange events that bedeviled a West German law office in 1967. At other times, light fixtures shattered or swung wildly (inset, right) in seeming response to the mere presence of office clerk Annemarie Schneider.

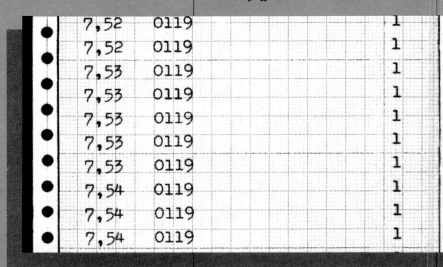

7,52	0119	1
7,52	0119	1
7,53	0119	1
7,53	0119	1
7,53	0119	1
7,53	0119	1
7,53	0119	1
7,54	0119	1
7,54	0119	1
7,54	0119	1

told Roll that the breakage "makes me feel happy. I don't know why."

By February of 1967, however, Laubheim's patience had shattered, and Vasquez was out of a job. Roll and Pratt invited the clerk to J. B. Rhine's laboratory in North Carolina for testing under controlled conditions. Though these sessions failed to produce results as dramatic as the warehouse incidents, the researchers believed

that Vasquez's poltergeist broke a vase in Rhine's office.

Back in Miami, Vasquez reportedly remained at the center of poltergeist activity. Unexplained disturbances followed him through a series of jobs and some close brushes with the law. But while Vasquez may have had his larcenous tendencies, he was never caught faking poltergeist activity in the warehouse. And if nothing else,

the circumstances persuaded Pratt. "I have no doubt," the investigator said, "that it was a genuine case."

The Clock-Watching Poltergeist

A few months later, across the Atlantic in Europe, a case involving another angry young clerk would prove no less perplexing. According to investigations conducted by the tireless Hans Bender and by a pair of British documentary filmmakers, it was in the summer of 1967 that attorney Sigmund Adam, in the Bavarian town of Rosenheim, noticed his telephones behaving in a most peculiar way. Incoming calls were interrupted by clicking noises or cut off. At other times all four of the office's extensions rang at once, although there was no one at the other end of the line.

For several weeks repairmen checked the building's wiring and Adam even had the telephones and their junction box replaced, but the disturbances persisted. In October Adam installed a meter to record all telephone activity in the office. To his astonishment, the meter instantly began registering calls, even though no one was using the phone. Dozens of undialed calls were logged in by the meter, and telephone company records revealed that nearly all had gone to the local time-of-day service. During one fifteen-minute period on October 20, forty-six telephone calls to the "talking clock" were recorded.

Technically, Adam knew, that was impossible. No one could complete that many calls in a quarter of an hour, even if the caller did not wait to hear the time. The telephone company shrugged and continued to present Adam with huge bills. The lawyer had his telephones replaced again. This time he put a lock on each phone so none of his employees could make a call without his permission. But the phantom clock watcher continued to dial the talking clock as enthusiastically as ever, placing as many as eighty calls in a single day.

Soon Adam's telephone troubles were to pale in comparison with his other problems. On October 20, the same day that the talking clock was being dialed continuously, every light in the office went out with a loud bang. A local electrician discovered that each fluorescent tube in the

hanging light fixtures had been twisted in its socket until it disconnected. But the electrician had no sooner replaced all the tubes than there was another loud bang and the office went dark again. And that was not all, the office staff informed the electrician: Sometimes the fuses simply ejected themselves.

After the wiring and electrical fixtures passed inspection, an engineer from the electricity board was asked to examine the electricity supply itself. A voltage meter, carefully sealed in order to prevent tampering, recorded a series of unusual fluctuations in the office power supply. Odder still, the power fluctuated only during office hours, never at night or on the weekend. "It is an energy quite beyond our comprehension," wrote the electrical engineer. Two physicists, from the prestigious Max Planck Institute, had to agree.

Meanwhile, fuses continued to pop and light bulbs to explode. The fluorescent tubes were replaced with ordinary bulbs, but they shattered, too, and one woman was cut by flying glass. To protect the staff members, Adam had nylon bags wrapped around each bulb to catch the debris. That precaution seemed to enrage whatever spirit plagued the office: The hanging light fixtures swung back and forth so violently that they dented the ceiling plaster, and framed paintings spun all the way around on their hooks.

The technical experts admitted defeat and packed up their gear. Once again, the field was left to Bender, who had investigated the earlier cases of the Schrey and Plach families. Bender soon became convinced that the law office was the haunt of a poltergeist and, guided by experience, looked about for its human focus. He found it immediately in nineteen-year-old Annemarie Schneider, one of the two young clerks. The voltage meter recorded its first zigzag when Schneider arrived for work each day, he noticed, and electric lights swung overhead as she walked down the corridors.

In many respects,

Schneider resembled Julio Vasquez and other suspected poltergeist agents. A psychologist who worked with Bender found that Schneider was emotionally unstable and desperately unhappy. Bender speculated that her constant feeling of frustration discharged itself through recurrent spontaneous psychokinesis. The repeated calls to the telephone time service may well have been an unconscious expression of the young woman's impatience to leave the office, Bender suggested, while the other manifestations may have arisen from her desire to relieve the tedium of her workday.

Although Schneider proved unable to generate any poltergeist activity in Bender's laboratory at the University of Freiburg, by that point the exercise was purely academic. As soon as she left Adam's office on sick leave, never to return, the reported disturbances ceased. But the poltergeist, if such it was, continued to dog her footsteps. It was blamed whenever anything went awry in subsequent jobs and for upsetting the electrical system at a bowling alley that she visited with her fiancé—thus ending the engagement. It finally left her only after Schneider married another man and had a child.

The Stones of Thornton Road

For all the technology brought to bear on the Rosenheim case and others, reported poltergeist activity itself has changed little over the centuries. In a way, the clicking noises that first disrupted lawyer Adam's telephone service are the modern equivalent of the persistent rapping that ushered in the disturbances at the Cideville parsonage in 1850. The case of the stone throwings on Thornton Road in Birmingham, England, provides an even louder echo of the past.

Phantom stone throwings are among the earliest and most frequent hallmarks of poltergeist activity. Records dating back to AD 858 show that the citizenry of a small

Residents of five houses on Thornton Road in Birmingham, England, covered their windows with boards or chicken wire as shields against the rocks with which their homes were bombarded in 1980.

German town on the Rhine thought that a malignant spirit was throwing stones against the walls of their houses. The same report might have been issued by the residents of five houses on Thornton Road—targets of almost nightly bombardments with large stones for several years in the early 1980s.

When the stone throwing began in 1981, the owners of the afflicted houses naturally assumed that the culprits were neighborhood children. But after months had passed without a child ever being caught in the act, they called in the police. Throughout the winter of 1981-1982, one of Britain's coldest, a special surveillance squad monitored Thornton Road with infrared scopes, image intensifiers, and automatic cameras; they tried to locate the points from which the stones might have been thrown based on their direction and allowing for the possible use of catapults and launchers. It was all to no avail.

By the end of 1982, the police had devoted more than 3,500 man-hours to the investigation, and the few clues they had found only increased their confusion. The stones that had bounced off the houses, they said, were entirely clean not only of fingerprints but of any trace of soil. Indeed, they appeared to have been washed.

The residents of Thornton Road settled in for the siege; some windows were boarded over, and others were covered with heavy chicken wire to blunt the impact of the stones. Then, like most cases in which a poltergeist has been suspected, the stone throwing simply ended, as inexplicably as it began. Some locals hypothesized that it was the work of someone who had a grudge against one family but, to conceal his identity, had stoned all five houses. It is an intriguing theory, but it still does not explain why no one was ever caught throwing stones.

Attack of the Killer Telephones

Catching a culprit red-handed does not always change the minds of those determined to see a poltergeist at work. That is true even when there is incontrovertible evidence of fraud, as in the case of the supposed poltergeist that dogged a Columbus, Ohio, family in 1984.

John and Joan Resch first attracted atten-

tion in late 1983, when a reporter for the *Columbus Dispatch* went to their home to chronicle the couple's extraordinary work with foster children. Over the years, the Resches had taken in more than 250 homeless children. At the time the article appeared, the family consisted of John and Joan, their son, Craig, their adopted daughter, Tina, and four foster children.

Five months later, the Resch family was in the news again but for a very different reason: Fourteen-year-old Tina had become the focus of a strange and frightening series of events. On a Saturday morning in March 1984, all the lights in the Resches' home went on at once, without anyone touching a switch. By evening, weirder things were happening: Lamps, brass candlesticks, and clocks flew through the air; wine glasses shattered; the shower ran on its own; and eggs rose out of their carton and dashed themselves against the ceiling. The focus of this madness seemed to be Tina, who even got smacked in the head by some of the airborne objects.

By Monday the Resch home had been visited by the police, members of the family's church, and the press. Although the house was a shambles of broken glass by that time, a photographer from the *Dispatch* found that each time he aimed his camera, the supposed poltergeist settled down. Finally, the cameraman made an elaborate show of being unprepared. The ruse worked. While Tina quietly sat in a chair a nearby telephone rose from the table, sailed across her lap, and was captured on film.

The publication of the photograph touched off a national media furor. Television crews and newspaper reporters crowded into the Resches' two-story frame house in the hope of witnessing further supernatural happenings. The ubiquitous investigator William Roll flew to Columbus to see the carryings-on firsthand. When a picture fell off its hook and Roll's own tape recorder flew seven feet, the earnest parapsychologist pronounced events the handiwork of a poltergeist.

Nonsense, said James Randi, the famous magician and escape artist who specializes in investigating, and often debunking, purportedly supernatural phenomena. The Resches had barred Randi from their

A newspaper photograph of Tina Resch, nearly grazed by a flying telephone, turned the fourteen-year-old into a celebrity in 1984. Other pictures showed her pulling the cord.

home, saying they feared intensification of the "circus atmosphere" that had already surrounded them. So Randi turned his attention to the roll of film shot by the *Dispatch* photographer that had sparked national attention.

The only frame that had been widely circulated was the one showing the telephone flying across Tina's lap. To Randi, though, the rest of the roll was more revealing: It showed Tina's hands in position to manipulate the telephone cord and base. Randi and his associates, convinced they had unmasked the culprit, jokingly dubbed the sequence "the attack of the flying killer telephones."

Soon there was even more damaging evidence. During an extended visit by reporters, a television camera that had accidentally been left running recorded the girl grasping a table lamp by its cord and jerking it toward her while letting out a cry of horror. For her part, Tina explained that she had become bored by the lengthy interviews and had hoped that the press would leave once it got its story. But for the skeptics, the film was proof positive of a poltergeist named Tina.

Yet not everybody shared that view. Many of the supposedly skeptical reporters remained sure that other seemingly supernatural events were genuine. Roll later conceded that he had not been observing under "controlled conditions," but he continued to assert that Tina seemed to have demonstrated genuine recurrent spontaneous psychokinesis. As for Tina, "I just want it to stop," she said.

Eventually it did, as all alleged poltergeist disturbances do. Whatever the truth about Tina, such finitude is a hallmark of the phenomenon—a quality, psychical researchers suggest, that may explain as much about poltergeists as does the activity itself. For the troubled human agents who are its focus, Alan Owen has suggested, the poltergeist is like a fever that runs its course. "We might guess that poltergeistery starts but eventually terminates," the researcher wrote, "because it is not a disease but a cure."

Strange happenings unnerve family

By Mike Harden
Dispatch columnist

At 9 a.m. last Saturday, the lights went on in the neat tract house in northern Columbus. In a home bustling with the activity of six children, such things rarely turn a head. But all the lights went on at once, all without a hand touching a switch.

John and Joan (they requested their last name be withheld) assumed the incident had been triggered by a power surge and telephoned the Columbus and Southern Ohio Electric Co. It was suggested that they call an electrician.

Electrical contractor Bruce Claggett was certain, when he arrived at the home not long after lunch, that it was simply a problem with the circuit breaker.

"I WAS UP there three hours," Claggett said, "and the lights were just turning themselves on all over the place." He tried taping the light switches.

"As fast as I would tape them in the down position, they'd come back on," the electrician said. Closet lights operated with a pull string would be extinguished, but seconds later they would be glowing again.

At 5:30 p.m. Claggett went home, unable to explain the phenomenon and half afraid to tell his wife what he had witnessed.

But by 5:30, it was not simply the lights. Small objects in the house had begun to move unaided by human touch: candles, lamps, wall hangings. Upstairs, the shower began running. The hands of clocks began turning much faster than normal.

A RATTLING picture on the family room wall was placed behind the couch, only to slide out three times.

"I don't believe in the supernatural," Joan said Monday, "but the stereo would blast, and radios and TVs would turn on without electricity."

As the weekend wore on, a pattern began to develop. The intensity and focus of what Joan had begun to identify as the "force" seemed to center upon the couple's 14-year-old daughter, Tina. It was she who was most often struck by flying objects: a brass candlestick, a clock, a wall hanging.

Near midnight Saturday, Columbus police were sum-

Dispatch photographer Fred Shannon took this picture of a telephone flying across Tina's lap. The phone had been on the table next to Tina. Shannon had seen other items move and caught this one on film

© Coypright 1984, The Dispatch Printing Co.

moned. There was nothing they could do.

WINE GLASSES shattered. Eggs, removed from the refrigerator, leaped from the stovetop and splattered on the ceiling. Knives flew from drawers. A chair tumbled after Tina as she crossed the living room, stopping only when it became wedged in a doorway.

The only respite from the strange events came on Sunday, in the morning when Tina left the house for church and again in the afternoon when she went out to visit a friend.

By Sunday evening, three elders from the Mormon Church had been summoned by a relative and, laying their hands upon Tina's head, attempted a prayer blessing to dispel the "force." It was to no avail.

By Monday morning, scarcely a glass was unbroken.

In the dining room, stemware lay shattered on the floor. In the living room, upturned furniture and a shattered picture were scattered about.

"I JUST want it to stop," Tina said. Yet, as she spoke, a telephone near her leaped through the air. She replaced it not once, but a half-dozen times. Each time, as stunned visitors watched, it would again fling itself across the room.

A cup of coffee flipped from a nearby table onto Tina's lap and then smashed against the fireplace. She moved to a love seat. An afghan on the floor lifted itself into the air and flopped over her.

Demons? Poltergeists?

Bill Roll, director of the Psychical Research Institute in Chapel Hill, N.C., and author of *The Poltergeist*, identified the problem as Recurrent Spontaneous Psychokinesis, or RSPK.

"IT REFERS," Roll explained, "to the ability, usually unconscious, to affect physical objects in the person's environment.

"It is frequently said that these occurrences are related to demons, but there is no substantiation for this. A number of people are going to say, 'Well, these people are mad.'"

Indeed, an Ohio State University psychology professor contacted about the incident suggested the journalist call North Carolina, adding in jest that it might even be possible to do so without dialing.

Roll said a half-dozen RSPK cases each year are usually documented in the United States. The median age of the victim, he said, is 14 (Tina's age). Nausea and headaches often accompany the onset of the phenomenon. Pent-up tension and psychological stress often trigger it, he said.

TINA HAS lately experienced both headaches and nausea. Joan, her adoptive mother, further acknowledged that lately there have been problems in the home stemming from Tina's conflicting feelings about her adoptive vs. biological parents.

The duration of RSPK is usually two months if the victim remains in the home, Roll said.

But by late Monday night, nerves frayed, exhausted by sleeplessness, John and Joan had gathered their children and moved into a motel. In their wake, they left a house of empty beds and silent rooms, its lights glowing strangely into the March night.

CHAPTER 2

Putting PK to the Test

sychology instructor Joseph Banks Rhine was at work in his office at Duke University one day early in 1934 when a stranger came to the door. Students often dropped in unannounced to chat with Rhine—but what this young man had to say was totally unexpected. Unceremoniously settling himself on a corner of Rhine's desk, he said, "Hey, doc, I've got something to tell you I think you ought to know." He then took Rhine into his confidence. Besides being a student, he was a professional gambler with an extraordinary talent: He could will the outcome of a dice throw.

This was news to make anyone sit up and take notice, especially an academician who pursued phenomena on the fringes of science. Rhine had attracted a great deal of attention both on campus and off for his investigation of extrasensory perception. Sure enough, he immediately asked for a demonstration. The pair squatted down, and while the gambler threw his dice on the office floor, Rhine kept track of the results. The gambler did not claim to have perfect control over the dice, and that day his success was only modest. He wielded the most influence, he told Rhine, when he was especially excited, confident, or anxious for a particular outcome.

That casual visit made enough of an impression to launch Rhine into a whole new field—the laboratory investigation of powers of mind over matter, which would interest him for the rest of his long and productive life. Over the following decades, other psychologists, physicists, engineers, biologists, and psychiatrists—along with a host of amateurs as well—would follow his investigative lead. They would produce thousands of scientific studies—and trigger a multitude of criticisms and indictments of their work.

From its beginning, the primary purpose of research into the field of mind over matter—or, as Rhine named it, psychokinesis—was to provide definitive proof that the phenomenon being investigated was real. As research progressed and became more sophisticated, students of PK would look for evidence of the nature and mechanics of what many believed to be a potent mental force. There was also a tantalizing, practical goal: Since any object, large or small, was theoretically subject to the effects of PK, the force seemed to have unlimited uses, if it could only be brought under control.

Reports of events that could be classified as PK phenomena are as old as the legends, myths, and scriptures of the world's most ancient cultures. Until the latter half of the nineteenth century, mysterious events such as levitating holy men or objects that moved spontaneously were not considered the stuff of scientific research. In the mid-1800s, the phenomenon known as spiritualism—the belief that people can communicate with the dead through a human intermediary, or medium—swept Europe and America, stirring up such a storm of interest that some scientists and academics began to perceive the possibilities of a fascinating new field of study. By 1882, a mixed group of British spiritualists and Cambridge University intellectuals banded together to form the Society for Psychical Research, an organization dedicated to the unbiased investigation of psychic phenomena. An American branch of the SPR sprang up soon afterward.

Along with other early psychical researchers, most members of the SPR and the ASPR tended more toward anecdote gathering than experimentation. They collected stories of the feats of mediums and offered rational explanations, but they did not investigate methodically or establish the conditions under which a particular event could be expected to occur. They did not, in proper scientific fashion, look for general principles, but tended instead to focus on the supposed uniqueness of each event. Their work generally took place on the mediums' home turf, often a darkened room where close observation was all but impossible.

Even so, these pioneering researchers did have considerable impact. For one thing, they made it at least marginally respectable to study psychokinetic phenomena. They also supported the idea that the force apparently exploited by the mediums was not necessarily the province of the spirits. Perhaps, they said, it was something that occurred naturally in humans and was subject to unconscious control, something that scientists should be able to detect and describe. In short, the early investigators outlined what was to be studied. But it remained for J. B. Rhine—frequently

in collaboration with his wife, Louisa—to develop what most observers consider to be the first systematic, experimental approach to psychokinetic phenomena.

Born in 1895 and schooled as a botanist, Rhine had been nudged toward parapsychology in 1922, when he attended a lecture by the British author Sir Arthur Conan Doyle, an avid dabbler in spiritualism. His interest was further piqued when he read a book by the British-born Harvard psychologist William McDougall, who contended that a full understanding of human nature required the study of psychic matters. In 1927, when McDougall was asked to set up a department of psychology at Duke, Rhine jumped at the chance to join him there to engage in psychic research.

At the time, such study was a wide-open field in the academic world. Rhine and McDougall were swimming against the tide of behaviorism, which accepted only strictly observable events as a proper subject for psychologists to study. The Duke investigators, however, shared with the psychic research societies an interest in the decidedly nonbehaviorist phenomenon of telepathy—the supposed ability of minds to communicate directly through channels other than the generally recognized senses.

Rhine decided to use his scientific training to investigate telepathy and the closely related phenomenon of precognition—the supposed capacity of an individual to foresee future events. Later, he would coin the term extrasensory perception, or ESP, to describe such abilities. The new name, he hoped, would help diminish the

prejudice against his research in academic circles. Instead of concerning himself with mediums or other superstars of the occult, Rhine sought evidence of ESP in ordinary people, usually student volunteers.

Conceptually, it was an easy transition for him from ESP to PK. If the mind could bypass the senses and know the world by some other mode of perception, he reasoned, it could conceivably bypass nerves and muscles to act on the physical world with some other sort of power. Rhine had long been fascinated by the idea of mind over matter but was unsure of how it could be tested. Thus, when the young gambler came to see him, he was instantly alert to the investigative possibilities of dice throwing, which could easily and inexpensively be adapted to laboratory experimentation and statistical analysis.

For his first experiments, Rhine recruited students as subjects and followed the gambler's procedure. A subject simply shook a pair of dice in cupped hands, threw them onto the floor, and let them rebound from a corner—all the while concentrating on rolling high numbers, which Rhine

defined as any combination of the dots on the two upper die faces adding up to eight or more. Six of the thirty-six possible combinations add up to seven, which he declared a neutral number. The remaining thirty combinations are evenly divided between high and low numbers. According to the laws of chance, fifteen out of every thirty-six throws, or five out of twelve, should come up high. For statistical convenience, Rhine divided his experimental sessions into twelve-throw units, which he called runs.

In each run, results governed by nothing but chance—which statisticians call the mean chance expectation, or MCE—should have produced five high combinations. With statistical analysis, Rhine could easily determine whether his subjects as a group were exceeding the MCE. By comparing the actual results of a run with the MCE, Rhine came up with a critical ratio that expressed how much, if at all, the results deviated from the MCE. He then computed the odds of coming up with that particular critical ratio. This computation produced a probability value, known as a p-value. For example, if the odds against a particular critical ratio were 100 to 1, the p-value would be 1 in 100, or .01.

The rule of thumb in any scientific undertaking is that a probability value of .05, or 5 in 100, shows a significant deviation from chance. Rhine knew that conventional standards would not be stringent enough to establish the credibility of his novel and controversial work. He chose a p-value of .01 as his standard: Only if the odds were 100 to 1 against the results of an experiment being pure chance would he call them significant.

Even applying this conservative

Concentrating on a specific number, a subject at J. B. Rhine's parapsychology laboratory at Duke University tries to influence dice thrown repeatedly from a cup. Researcher Elizabeth Humphrey (left) concluded that the success rate was highest in the earliest throws.

p-value, his subjects appeared to have phenomenal influence over the dice. In fact, the first series of 562 runs resulted in a p-value of one in over a billion. Rhine was much impressed by this start, but he was also cautious: He could not be certain that the scores were because of PK and not some hidden factor in the experiment. One possibility was that his subjects were unusually skillful throwers who could manually guide the fall of the dice, even when they used a dice cup instead of their cupped hands.

To eliminate any effect of throwing techniques, Rhine designed a crude but serviceable dice chute consisting of a board with a corrugated surface—to make the dice bounce a bit—and two nails sticking out near the top. The chute was propped at a forty-five-degree angle on a cushioned chair, a ruler was placed across the two nails, and the dice were set on the ruler. While the subject concentrated on achieving a high score, Rhine lifted the ruler and let the dice tumble down the chute. Somewhat to his surprise, the scores of the first 108 runs conducted with the dice board were just as high as those of the hand-tossed series.

Rhine followed up with another device for testing the influence of throwing skills: a "dice machine," composed of a rectangular wire-mesh cage fitted with baffles and mounted at midpoint on an axis. A small motor rotated the cage, sending the dice tumbling over the baffles until it was shut off and the dice came to rest. Rhine and two assistants took turns operating the machine and serving as subjects, trying to achieve a high score. When playing the subject role, they chose the speed at which the cage turned but were not allowed to

touch either the dice or the machine. Once again, Rhine was surprised by the results: Scores in machine-thrown runs were slightly higher than runs in which subjects used a dice cup. Perhaps, he speculated, the novelty of the machine, or the fact that subjects had nothing to do but concentrate on making a hit, gave the scores a boost.

Another possible hidden factor that Rhine had to screen out was "dice bias"—an uneven distribution of weight in a die, possibly due to the indentations on each side, that could cause a particular side to land faceup more often than the rest. Methodically, Rhine tested for bias by using differently constructed dice. One type had smooth surfaces and painted dots, another had inlaid dots. No matter which type of dice was used, however, the experiments continued to show evidence in support of psychokinesis, and Rhine concluded that dice bias was not a significant problem in the research.

But one effort to screen for dice bias produced curious results. In some runs, Rhine changed the target combination from high numbers to either sevens or low numbers.

As J. B. Rhine keeps score, a subject concentrates on the number that comes up after dice tumble down a board. Such techniques, used to prevent subjects from skewing the outcome by handling the dice, produced results similar to those of dice thrown by hand.

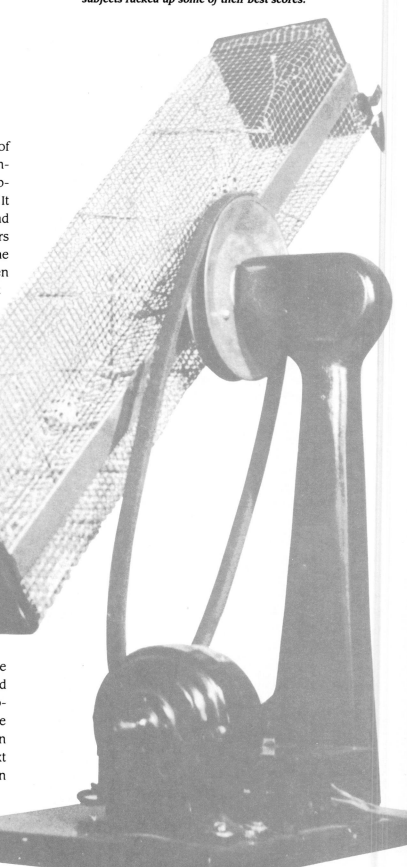

The sevens series yielded notable results, with a p-value of 3 in 10,000. But in the runs where the target was low numbers, the overall scores were actually below the MCE. Subjects had done *worse* than chance would have dictated. It seemed to Rhine that a prejudice against low numbers had developed during the first experiments, when high numbers were always the desired target. Combinations yielding the sum of seven seemed to be an acceptable target, but when low numbers became the target, the subjects were not able to overcome their acquired prejudice. Their inner feeling about the target, it appeared, had caused PK to operate in a negative way.

The target-switching series provided a fascinating glimpse of what would later come to be called psi-missing—the alleged ability of a subject to unconsciously deflect PK in order to miss a target. (This effect is also said to occur in ESP.) But psi-missing was only one hint of something that was becoming increasingly clear to Rhine. The gambler's claim that his throwing ability varied with his mood was apparently true of Rhine's laboratory subjects as well. Gamelike, informal conditions and enthusiastic subjects produced good results, while negative feelings produced chance or worse-than-chance results.

Two years of experiments and thousands of dice throws had made Rhine confident that he was on the road to documenting the existence of psychokinesis. Far less apparent, however, were the nature and mechanics of the purported force that made the phenomenon possible. In hopes of learning something about that force, Rhine next examined the influence of certain physiological factors on PK performance. These factors had produced a decided effect on scores in tests of extrasensory perception; physical depression deliberately induced with doses of the barbiturate sodium amytal seemed to lower test scores, whereas stimulation with caffeine appeared to raise them.

Now Rhine decided to test the effects of another depressant, alcohol, on PK. Rhine and his graduate assistant, Richard L. Averill, each downed a hefty 3.5 ounces of gin with an equal amount of ginger ale and waited twenty minutes for the alcohol to take effect. After several runs with the dice, Averill began to feel queasy, then vomited. He resolutely continued with the experiment and for the last part of the test felt little effect of the gin. His final score was only fractionally lower than that of the prealcohol run. Rhine was a better subject: He kept his liquor down and completed his throws without mishap. But while he had scored impressively for PK while sober, he scored at a level below chance when tipsy.

Even so, Rhine conceded that it was impossible to be sure that alcohol alone had impaired his performance. Possibly, he noted, the cause could have been the mere expectation or suggestion that alcohol would hinder PK. Equally ambiguous were the results of another drug experiment two days later, when his and Averill's scores leaped after they had caffeine-rich cola drinks.

Experiments such as the series in which he switched targets from high dice to low dice, plus the reports of his test subjects, had convinced Rhine that psychological factors such as mood or the need to succeed had a tremendous impact on PK. But proving it was another thing, for these factors are subjective and extremely difficult, if not impossible, to measure, interpret, compare, and control in a convincingly scientific manner. At best, Rhine could only develop a general understanding of the mental states that enhanced or hindered a subject's supposed PK abilities.

More evidence came, however, in an informal test involving two of Rhine's research assistants, Margaret Price and Joseph L. Woodruff, who was also a star PK subject. Price bet Woodruff that she could sabotage his scores if she made negative comments in the room as he sought to influence the fall of dice in the machine. Her written report to Rhine did not detail exactly what she said or did, but Woodruff's scores, which had been extraordinarily good the previous day, plummeted to an abysmal below-chance level.

To be sure, this test was far from airtight. For one thing, no one except Woodruff and Price was present at the time. But it suggested a fascinating implication for psychic research: Anyone present at any experiment, particularly a negative observer, might be at least partially responsible for the outcome. If PK were subject to both conscious and unconscious control, it would be extremely difficult to prove who, if anyone, was actually determining the events in an experimental setting. This inherent ambiguity made it difficult to answer criticism that no experiment could ever show conclusively where the supposed force originated. In the future, every PK researcher would try to overcome this stumbling block by clever experimental design.

Rhine's experiments in PK ground to a halt with World War II, when many members of the psychology department joined the armed forces or left for war-related civilian jobs. With a dearth of subjects and assistants, Rhine decided in 1942 that the time was ripe to review and analyze his eight years of research on PK, and he pulled out his old files. His ESP experiments had often shown that subjects did better at the beginning and end of a test than they did in the middle—results that, when charted, produced a U-shaped curve

After a dose of sodium amytal, a subject at Duke nods drowsily over a test of her psychokinetic abilities. According to researchers, large amounts of the narcotic lowered performance, but small doses seemed to improve it.

known as a position effect. Rhine had interpreted that pattern as strong evidence that ESP is a genuine mental process, since known processes such as recall have the same tendency to peak at the beginning and end of a test, and slump in between. Psychologists had concluded that performance declines when a subject begins to get bored with the experimental task.

Perhaps, Rhine speculated, similar patterns would appear in the records of his PK research. And as he and his one remaining wartime graduate student, Elizabeth Humphrey, sorted through the old experiment reports, it did not take them long to discover a position effect. In each of eighteen reports they compared, the subjects made more hits early in a run than they did later, and the earliest runs in a test sequence also showed higher scores than later runs. Another analysis yielded a U curve in nine of the eighteen reports. Rhine's wife and frequent research associate, Louisa Rhine, later compared the effect to a "gardener hoeing long rows, who would find the end of a row endowed with added interest just because it was the end." To the Rhines, the results were persuasive evidence that PK was a genuine mental process.

And J. B. Rhine was ready to respond to whatever barbs the critics of parapsychology might hurl at him or his work. In March 1943, the Rhines jointly published the results of the early high-dice experiments in the *Journal of Parapsychology,* which Rhine had cofounded with his colleague William McDougall in 1937, a year before McDougall's death. Over the next three years he published the rest of his PK research. And, to his amazement, he was not greeted by an immediate, hostile outcry from conventional psychologists and other expected naysayers. Perhaps, he thought, the critics did not know—at least for the moment—how to respond to the quantitative and statistical approach he had used to study a subject that had historically been the stuff of breathless anecdote.

Indeed, his work drew numerous positive responses, scientific and otherwise. In a letter to Rhine, the English novelist Aldous Huxley wrote, "I admire you for not going mad under the strain of devising scientific experiments in a field where there is no really satisfactory hypothesis!" More muted praise came from English criminologist and psychic researcher D. J. West. While noting that Rhine's procedures were rather informal and doubting that his results could be repeated by other experimenters, West conceded that the American's statistics were the most conclusive evidence to date for the existence of PK.

est had raised a key issue that would continue to dog Rhine and other researchers in parapsychology. One of the basic tenets of science is that experimental results claimed by one researcher cannot be accepted unless the same experiments carried out by other investigators produce the same results. A scientist might claim, for example, that water was used to fuel an internal combustion engine. But the world at large will not believe this unless other researchers are able to duplicate the feat.

And just as West suspected, Rhine's apparent successes proved difficult to repeat in experiments conducted by other researchers. In England, for example, a series of similar dice-throwing studies undertaken not long after Rhine published his findings failed to yield any indication of PK in action. Another set of experiments, conducted by a Philadelphia biophysicist in 1944, also showed no evidence of PK. While few critics have gone so far as to charge researchers such as Rhine with outright fraud, others have questioned their methods. The Brooklyn College psychologist Edward Girden, for example, carefully assessed Rhine's dice studies and faulted them for, among other things, their informal nature and lack of accurate recordkeeping.

Nonetheless, Rhine's methods continued to inspire other researchers to launch their own controlled studies of PK. Some used dice, as Rhine had; others, notably the German experimenter Sigurd R. Binski, used coins, with heads or tails the specified target on which subjects concentrated. In the first phase of his 1950 study, Binski simply asked each of his 117 subjects to drop a large handful of ten-pfennig coins onto a table while willing a specified face to come up. Their aggregate scores were a little better than chance, but not enough to be significant. One subject, however, a teenager named Kastor Seibel, had outstanding scores.

Binski wanted to do follow-up tests with Kastor, but the boy's widowed mother had become deeply alarmed by the testing. She feared that her son had inherited the supposed family trait of second sight—the ability to foretell events, especially tragic ones. When the last male in her line died on the very day he had predicted, Mrs. Seibel and her late husband agreed never to tell Kastor about the power he might share with his forebears. And until he participated in Binski's experiments, Kastor had never demonstrated any talent for the paranormal. Binski overcame Mrs. Seibel's objections and persuaded her to let the boy continue with the testing. He proceeded to turn in an astonishing performance, reportedly achieving scores that could not

have come about by chance even once in 10 billion times.

Cambridge University psychologist Robert H. Thouless began with coins but then abandoned them as he sought a way to test his hypothesis that there existed a single paranormal phenomenon—one composed of a motor aspect, or PK, as well as a cognitive ESP aspect—for which he and a colleague, B. P. Wiesner, had coined the popular term *psi.* In 1947, Thouless came up with a novel method of looking for this combined form of psychokinesis and extrasensory perception. He created a new type of experiment in which the target was "blind"; that is, subjects would not know in advance what result they should try to produce.

For his experiment, Thouless made six different cards, each with dots that corresponded to one of the six faces of a die. Without looking, he placed the cards facedown and then tossed four dice simultaneously for each card. Only after he had thrown for all six cards and recorded the results

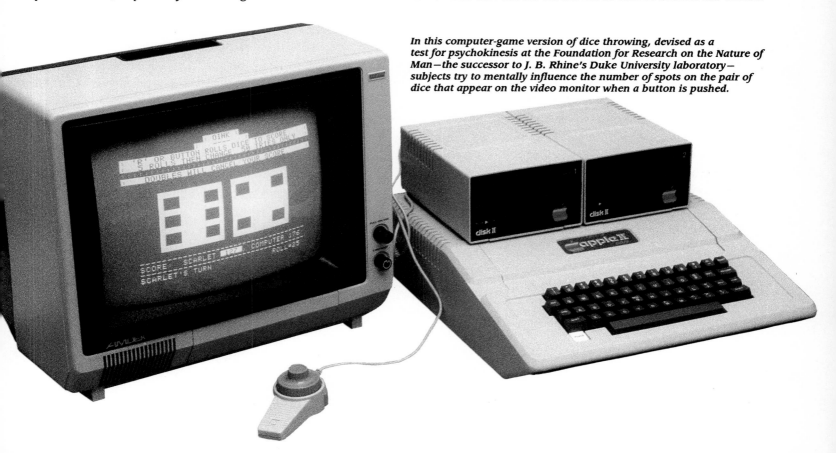

In this computer-game version of dice throwing, devised as a test for psychokinesis at the Foundation for Research on the Nature of Man—the successor to J. B. Rhine's Duke University laboratory— subjects try to mentally influence the number of spots on the pair of dice that appear on the video monitor when a button is pushed.

did he turn the cards over to compare them with the dice throws. Presumably, a match of cards and dice meant that he had divined the identity of the card through ESP and then controlled the fall of the dice through PK.

In fact, Thouless proved to be a better innovator than subject; his scores were only slightly better than chance. But two members of Britain's Society for Psychical Research soon reported remarkable success in blind-target experiments that added the element of distance. They first selected a die face, based on a random toss. Then, on ten given days, they asked ten subjects who were as many as 300 miles from the target to throw a pair of dice 100 times and mail a record of their results to the researchers. The subjects matched the target so often that, according to the published report, the odds were 4,000 to 1 against chance alone being responsible for their success.

At about the same time, two other researchers, working independently, introduced a new twist in Rhine's dice-throwing experiment: They wanted to see if subjects could use PK to cause dice or other objects to land in a target location. One of the innovators was Sigurd Binski, who used for his tests a standard roulette wheel with slots painted alternately red and black. Binski pushed the wheel to set it spinning and then tossed a small marble onto the whirling surface. When the wheel began to slow down, the bouncing marble came to rest in one of the slots. The experimenter had previously given his subjects a target color, red or black, and asked them to will the ball to fall into a slot of that color. Once again, Kastor Seibel was his star subject, racking up scores comparable with those he had achieved at coin tossing.

In the meantime, William E. Cox, a businessman and parapsychologist who put in a lot of time in Rhine's laboratory, had also been carrying out psychokinetic "placement" tests. His first such experiments, performed with volunteer subjects in 1946, involved the use of the lid of a typewriter case, dice, and a dice cup. He drew lines on the lid to divide it into 252 squares and gave each square a number from one to six; no contiguous squares received the same number. For each run, Cox would assign a subject a group of target squares—all the number-six squares, for example. The subject then upended a cup containing twenty-four dice while willing them to land on the target squares.

Over time, the apparent cumulative successes of his subjects convinced Cox that PK could somehow maneuver an object into a desired spot. But Cox was puzzled by test series that produced lower-than-chance results. Perhaps, he theorized, the dice were, in effect, loaded.

Behind that tentative conclusion was a debate that had been simmering in parapsychological circles for several years. At issue were the relative merits of two hypothetical descriptions of PK. According to the so-called loading hypothesis, PK is a force acting from within an object throughout the course of a run. It exerts itself in a steady and predictable manner, rather like familiar forces such as momentum or gravity. Proponents of the loading hypothesis believed that PK would ultimately turn out to be a phenomenon that would not be in conflict with the principles of physics. In contrast, the kinetic hypothesis described psychokinesis as a force external to an object, a force that exerts itself over a very short time-span—like a kick delivered to a soccer ball, for example.

Cox set about designing an elaborate experiment to test whether certain dice varied in their inherent responsiveness to psi. Some of them, he thought, might respond positively, hitting their targets with more regularity than did dice with an inherently negative response. He came up with a six-foot-high, three-tiered contraption in which he could closely observe the fall of the dice onto target areas. Results were ambiguous, however, and Cox moved on to another area of investigation—the possible relationship between PK and the number of simultaneous targets.

Over the years, researchers had noted a peculiar tendency in PK dice experiments: the greater the number of targets, the stronger the evidence of psychokinesis. Parapsychologists had no satisfactory explanation, though many of them thought that subjects found multiple targets more engaging than single ones and were thus more likely to

Games of Chance

For thousands of years before parapsy-chologists used dice to test for psychoki-nesis, gamblers were using the numbered cubes in games of chance. While most modern gamesters have abandoned the ancient notion that the fall of the dice is controlled by the gods, the belief that one can consciously affect the outcome of the throw of dice—or the turn of a roulette wheel or the images that come up on a slot machine *(right)*—continues to draw players to casinos the world over.

Most scientists would say that probabil-ity alone determines whether a player is going to win or lose. The branch of mathematics called probability theory predicts what may be expected to happen, on average, as a result of chance. For example, a player seeking to roll double sixes in dice is faced with odds of thirty-five to one. That is, in thirty-six rolls, the double six will, on average, come up once. And when someone beats awesome odds—one billion to one, for example—the theory explains that, statistically, it was bound to happen— albeit only once in every 1,000,000,001 times.

One of the most famous examples of this iron law of averages at work is the hero of the once-popular song, "The Man That Broke the Bank at Monte Carlo." An obscure Englishman, Charles Wells, became an overnight celebrity in 1891 when he emptied the bank at a casino roulette table of about $20,000—a considerable sum at the time—and then defied the odds by doing it again. But the rest of the story did not inspire a songsmith. Eventually Wells went back to the tables, where he lost all of his winnings and much more. Later impris-oned for fraud, the man who broke the bank died penniless.

summon their PK powers. Whatever the cause, Cox decided to explore a situation with an enormous number of targets.

For his new placement experiment, Cox chose the billions of sodium and chloride ions in an electrolytic solution as targets for PK. He asked subjects, in effect, to change the resistance of the saline solution to an electric current passed through it. To measure the changes, he hooked an electric stopwatch through a series of low-voltage relays to a pair of electrodes submerged in the saline solution. Cox asked his subjects to will the sodium and chloride ions to cling to the electrodes, thus slowing the sweep of the experimental stopwatch's hand or, alternatively, to will the ions to avoid the electrodes and hence speed up the stopwatch. In order to gauge a subject's effectiveness, Cox compared the difference in elapsed time between the test stopwatch and a second stopwatch used as a control. One group of subjects attained very high scores, with an overall probability value of 7 in 10,000.

Still, Cox was not ready to conclude that the subjects were actually propelling ions toward or away from the electrodes. If PK was really operating, he reasoned, it might be affecting some other part of the experimental setup. Hoping to determine the actual site of the effect, he rerouted the electrical circuit to bypass the saline solution. Subjects were given exactly the same instructions as before—and produced the same results.

Having all but ruled out influence on the ions, Cox made other attempts to pinpoint the possible sites of action. He asked subjects to concentrate first on the stopwatch hands, then on the current flowing through the low-voltage relays to the watches; in both cases, he detected evidence of a PK effect. In the end, though, he was left no closer than he had been at the outset in definitively pinning down whether and where PK was active, nor had he found how the supposed force might be affected by the number of targets.

Rhine, Binski, and Cox were not alone in using dice in hopes of finding the secrets of PK. Shortly after Cox had started experimenting with placement PK at Rhine's labora-

tory, Rhine received a letter from a noted Scandinavian electrical engineer, Haakon Forwald, reporting the success he and a group of fellow engineers had had with table tipping. Rhine replied that if Forwald wanted to investigate psychokinesis, he should abandon such séance standbys for a laboratory setup where controls and statistical evaluation would lend credence to his work.

By 1949, Forwald was working with dice, too. Although his experiments were patterned on the work done at Duke, his orientation was clearly determined by his background in engineering and physical science. He focused on explaining PK phenomena in terms of physical laws and was much less prone than the Duke researchers to include any possible psychological factors. Forwald also rejected the standard Duke practice of having different people serve as subject and experimenter. He was a loner and, in most instances, was his own subject.

For someone with 500 patents to his credit, Forwald put together a surprisingly primitive apparatus that consisted of nothing more than a dice trough, a slanted runway, a rimmed dice table, and a release mechanism. Pressing a push button at the end of a cord freed the trough so that it dropped and let the dice tumble down the runway to the table. Forwald divided the dice table into two target areas, labeled A and B, and concentrated on establishing mental contact with the dice before pushing the release button.

He reported spectacular results, with a probability value of one in a million. In subsequent years he introduced variables into his studies, using cubes of equal size but made of materials—wood, paper, aluminum, Bakelite, and steel—with different textures and weights. According to Forwald, he discovered after thousands of "throws," or releases of his dice trough, that his scores with lightweight dice were no higher than those with heavier ones; PK, he concluded, apparently does not conform to the law of physics stipulating that the lighter an object is, the greater the effect a given force will have on it.

Forwald noted another intriguing effect as well. In his so-called A-B order, in which he willed cubes to hit the A

target in the set first and then, in subsequent throws, the B target, he recorded far higher scores than he did in sets where he willed the B-A sequence. Alerted to this odd feature, he began to watch for it in a new series of throws and found that when he thought about his preference for the A-B order, the effect simply evaporated. But when he did not think about it, it just as mysteriously reappeared. Although Forwald had professed himself rather indifferent to any psychological factors that might underlie PK, he now concluded that an unconscious preference was apparently having an impact on his scores.

In 1957, Forwald came to Duke for a two-month visit with Rhine and his associates. He had worked alone for so long—almost always producing scores that appeared to be very strong evidence of PK—that it seemed the time had come to perform his experiments for friendly observers. And when he did, he had an embarrassing surprise that, for a time, called into question the remarkable scores he had been reporting from his one-man Swedish laboratory.

Despite his experiences with the A-B and B-A sequences, Forwald continued to downplay the psychological component of PK. But the Duke researchers were concerned that a radical change of environment and test conditions would lower Forwald's scores. The novelty of having a stranger looking on, they thought, might throw him off his accustomed stride. And sure enough, when Forwald went through his experimental paces with a series of individual observers, his scores were no better than chance would have predicted. Finally a secretary at the lab, Peggy Murphy, who was the wife of a Duke graduate biology student, stepped into the observer role. Forwald apparently felt comfortable with her, for his scores soared.

Having demonstrated his techniques at Duke, Forwald returned to Sweden, where he again became engrossed in studying the way a cube's surface would affect PK. He was certain that he could prove a relationship between the thickness of a cube's outer layer and the energy required to send it on a given trajectory. The distance a cube moved, he speculated, would show a clear relationship to the atomic weight of the metal used. For his experiments, he compared cubes coated with varying thicknesses of aluminum, copper, cadmium, silver, and lead. His new hypothesis was that PK somehow liberated a force from the atoms of a cube's surface material. As in the past, however, his experimentation led him up a blind alley. Neither a Geiger counter nor other measuring apparatus turned up evidence of atomic decay or magnetism—nor could Forwald prove his next hypothesis, that gravity might be the force mobilized from within by psychokinesis.

In the end, parapsychologists were divided over For-

Psychic Snapshots

One of the most intriguing areas of psychokinesis is thoughtography, in which images are said to be imprinted on photographic film by the mind alone. Perhaps the most famous and controversial of the thoughtographers was Ted Serios, a hard-drinking, unemployed bellhop from Chicago who during the 1960s claimed to produce snapshots of what was on his mind.

To take his thoughtographs, Serios sat in front of a Polaroid camera—favored because it provided quick results and precluded accusations of film tampering in the darkroom. Then, with great shows of physical exertion *(below),* he concentrated on a mental image of an existing picture while someone snapped the camera's shutter. His only prop was a so-called gizmo, a small cardboard or plastic tube that he held in front of the lens. He used it, he explained, to keep his fingers from obscuring the lens.

The usual result was an out-of-focus picture of Serios's face. Sometimes, though, the camera yielded totally black pictures, as if no light had entered the lens. At other times, the pictures developed were completely white, as if the film had been exposed to a very bright light. And then, there was the occasional thoughtograph, such as a blurry print of a building—sometimes only its tower or dome—that Serios had chosen earlier from a book or postcard.

Skeptics such as James Randi, the professional stage magician who has made a second career of debunking the allegedly paranormal, suggested that Serios could mount a photographic transparency on a tiny lens concealed on the inside of the gizmo. He could then hold the gizmo close to the camera, take a picture, slip the transparency into his pocket, and present the empty cylinder for inspection.

Supporters of Serios—who has since given up thoughtography—noted that he was never caught cheating and that he did not always use the gizmo. Then, too, certain discrepancies between the original photographs and his thoughtographs, such as misspelled names on buildings, indicated that any fraud would have to have been well planned. And not all thoughtographers have worked like Serios; in the 1970s, for example, a Japanese named Masuaki Kiyota produced a number of such snapshots while the cap was on the lens. But not even thoughtography's believers claim to know how it works. One notion is that thoughtographers use psychic force to manipulate the chemical particles on the film; another hypothesis is that they create an invisible image that the camera somehow captures on film.

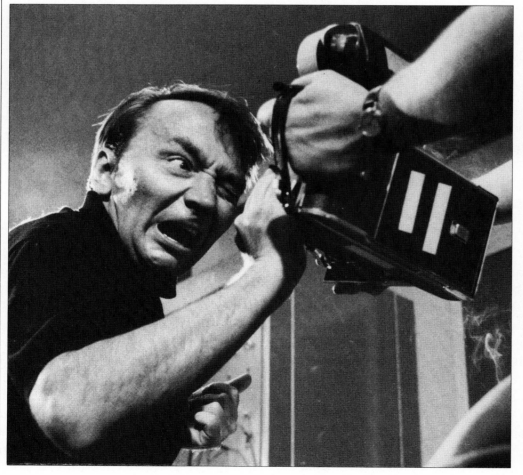

Two of Ted Serios's thoughtographs—shown against a background of the photograph he had seen earlier—reveal parts of Trajan's Column in Rome (bottom right) and the dome of the Church of Santa Maria di Loreto (top right), which is across the square.

wald's credibility. Some saw him as a serious investigator; others suspected that he was a well-meaning but bumbling amateur who was not above fudging his data to show results that were more wishful than real. Many from both camps, however, gave him and W. E. Cox credit for pioneering the probe into the ions and atoms of the microphysical world in their investigations of PK effects.

It was not until the 1960s, however, that this concept of so-called micro-PK came into its own. Previous dice and cube studies had suggested that randomly moving objects were more susceptible to the influence of psychokinesis than were stationary ones. Now, some researchers pushed the idea a little further and proposed that the more random and unpredictable the movement, the more powerful a PK effect would be.

To test their notions, they turned to the principles of atomic physics to investigate the most random of movements—those of subatomic particles emitted during the process of radioactive decay. Among those who took an interest in this approach was the German-born physicist Helmut Schmidt, who eventually left the Boeing Research Laboratories in Seattle, Washington, to work with J. B. Rhine in Durham and later moved on to the Mind Science Foundation of San Antonio, Texas, a research group founded by millionaire oilman Tom Slick.

Among Schmidt's first and most important contributions to micro-PK research were the ingenious high-speed electronic devices he designed and built. His random event generator, or REG—first used to test for ESP—is essentially an electronic coin-flipper in which the "coin" is an oscillating switch with two positions—positive, equivalent to heads in a coin toss, and negative, equivalent to tails. The switch is driven by the completely random—and, presumably, uncontrollable—emission of electrons from a bit of strontium 90 as the unstable element decays.

For one series of experiments, Schmidt connected the generator to a display panel with nine lights. At any given moment, only one light would be on. If the generator relayed a "heads" signal to the panel, the next light in a clockwise direction would light up; a "tails" signal would prompt a move counterclockwise. Electrons moving in a purely random way would, theoretically, make the lights flash on and off in an equally random pattern. But if PK could influence the way the radioactive material emitted electrons, the lights would display a discernible pattern. Schmidt asked subjects simply to concentrate on the light panel and try to make the bulbs light up sequentially in a clockwise direction. All of his early subjects did a bit better than pure chance would predict, according to Schmidt. But he reported that one of them, who believed herself to be psychic, was so good that the odds against her performance being the result of pure chance were a billion to one.

In a variation of this test, Schmidt substituted sound for light. Through headphones, subjects listened to clicks produced by electron emissions. They were instructed to concentrate on "hearing" more clicks in their right ear. The results were well above chance.

Schmidt's findings were intriguing, and his testing process seemed to eliminate some of the ambiguities that confused—or, critics alleged, tainted—earlier investigations of PK. His data could be automatically recorded and analyzed, reducing the chance for human error, bias, or fraud. On the other hand, some observers have maintained that these factors cannot be completely ruled out in the case of Schmidt's studies. They have further noted that some of the researcher's target generators could well have shown natural deviations from random patterns, deviations that could have been interpreted as evidence of PK. Moreover, the British psychologist and psi critic C. E. M. Hansel has pointed out that earlier tests by the U.S. Air Force, using a random target generator called VERITAC, turned up no evidence that the experimental subjects were exercising any kind of psi powers.

Whatever its flaws, Schmidt's work was part of a new direction in parapsychology. This movement tried to explain psi phenomena through a relatively new branch of physics known as quantum mechanics, which involved the study of subatomic particles.

Parapsychologists in the past had tried but failed to demonstrate conclusively that a known physical force underlay psychokinesis. During the nineteenth century and into the twentieth, electromagnetism was a strong candidate, and Forwald thought psychokinesis might be related to gravity. No one, however, had mustered evidence demonstrating that supposed parapsychological phenomena were governed by any of the known laws of physics. Now, looking to the microphysical world of quantum mechanics for their explanations, science-minded parapsychologists developed what they called "observation theories" that considered both PK and ESP as large-scale quantum events that

might feasibly be reconciled with this new realm of physics.

Quantum mechanics describes a seemingly chaotic state in which a subatomic particle exists at any given moment not as a bit of matter with a specific position, electrical charge, or direction, but merely as a so-called wave function whose characteristics can be described only as probabilities. But this state changes when an observer steps into the picture and measures the particle: The very act of measurement causes the wave function to collapse and the particle to "jump" from the quantum state in which it is a bundle of probabilities, to another quantum state in which it has a definite value. It is an odd world, a place where

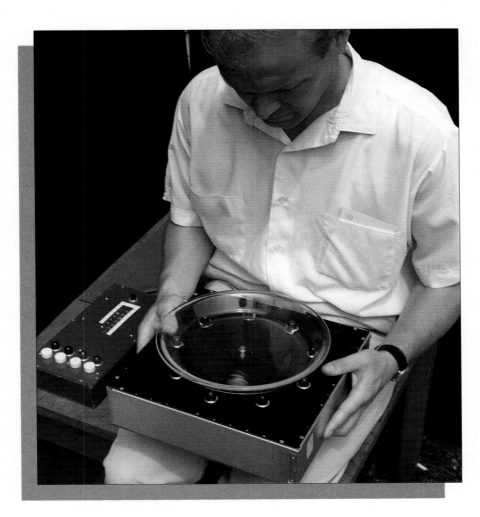

In a test designed by psi researcher Helmut Schmidt, a subject rocks a little ball around a glass pie dish as an aid to concentration while he tries to make the bulbs light up in a clockwise direction.

chance encounters have a supreme importance. Martin Gardner, a science writer—and a confirmed skeptic when it comes to the claims of parapsychology—likens the observer-measurer to an autocratic baseball umpire who declares, "Some is balls and some is strikes, but until I calls 'em they ain't nothing."

Although this implies an appalling anarchy in the physical world, there is a kind of order. Statistical probability suggests that a particle, such as an electron, will follow a particular course under given circumstances—although its movement lacks the statistical certainty of, say, the rebound of a billiard ball moving at a certain angle and speed. Large groups of particles are even more likely than single particles to behave in accordance with the laws of probability. Like a restaurateur who cannot be sure what an individual diner will order but has a fairly accurate idea of how many of each menu item a whole evening's worth of customers will order, the physicist can make fairly reliable predictions about the behavior of great numbers of particles.

The crucial impact of the observer on quantum phenomena seemed, to some parapsychologists, to offer an explanation of the relationship between PK and the physical world. Indeed, the Austrian physicist Erwin Schrödinger, one of the principal architects of quantum theory, seemed to be linking the psychic and physical when he wrote, "I—I in the widest meaning of the word, that is to say, every conscious mind that has ever said or felt 'I'—am the person, if any, who controls the 'motion of the atoms' according to the Laws of Nature." And Carl Jung, the great Swiss psychologist who collaborated with Nobel laureate and quantum physicist Wolfgang Pauli on a book titled *Interpretation of Nature and Psyche,* once observed that "the microphysical world of the atom exhibits certain features whose affinities with the psychic have impressed themselves even on the physicists. Here, it would seem, is at least a suggestion of how the psychic process could be 'reconstructed' in another medium, in that, namely, of the microphysics of matter."

No less a physicist than Albert Einstein put forth the idea that the behavior of quantum systems is governed by a unique set of factors—he called them "hidden variables" because they are not measurable factors like energy or mass. It is these variables, in the view of observation theorists such as Helmut Schmidt, that allow all quantum events to interact with one another irrespective of space and time. And in the mid-1970s, Schmidt devised a series of experiments to search for evidence of "retro-PK"—that is, a form of supposed psychokinesis that could move backward across the barriers of time and, in effect, influence events that had already occurred.

This intriguing research had its beginnings in a more conventional PK experiment in which Schmidt used one of his random generators to produce a random sequence of clicks, barely audible to subjects through their headphones. By chance alone, subjects could expect to hear a click once in about 6.4 seconds.

Schmidt speculated that some of his subjects might be able to speed up the clicks through PK, but he did not ask them to try. Instead, his only instruction was to listen very carefully, so as not to miss any of the faint clicks, and to imagine a vaguely analogous real-life experience, such as walking in a forest and listening for soft bird calls. What Schmidt hoped to create was a mood of eager anticipation, a condition that Rhine and other researchers had maintained is conducive to PK success. Apparently, it worked. Schmidt reported that his subjects heard clicks every 5.42 seconds—almost a full second ahead of the chance schedule. Without even consciously trying, it seemed, his subjects had somehow altered the timing of the hits.

Now came Schmidt's move into retro-PK. He activated his equipment to record the clicks on audio cassettes. Neither he nor anyone else was present when the recordings were made, and, he reported, no one listened to the tapes until the subjects heard them during the experiment. According to observation theory, the recordings were at that point unmeasured, since no one had heard them, and their characteristics were only probabilities and not certainties—although it could be argued that the clicks were, in fact, measured and set in reality when they were taped. Schmidt selected half the recordings as targets for the subjects and designated the other half as controls.

He then assembled his subjects and described the same procedure used for the first experiment. He did not tell them that they were listening to prerecorded sequences, since conventional ideas of time would make ridiculous the notion that they could change past events. But when he compared the experimental tapes with the control tapes, he discovered that the ones that the subjects had listened to had significantly shorter intervals between clicks. It appeared that his subjects had achieved the impossible: They

apparently exercised PK to alter events—in this case, recorded sounds—that had already taken place. For observation theorists, the experiment seemed a major triumph, although critics would maintain that the results, like so many findings reported by parapsychologists, were inconclusive and unrepeatable by other researchers.

Helmut Schmidt's elaborate equipment was a far cry from J. B. Rhine's homemade dice-throwing apparatus, but the two researchers had the same modest goal. They were looking for PK in ordinary people, not in those claiming unusual gifts, and were satisfied with tiny, unspectacular effects, often detectable only in statistics extracted from many experiments. Like a number of other parapsychologists, they had done their best to remove PK from the realm of the occult and to make it as impersonal and scientific as possible.

In the 1970s, however, just when Schmidt and his colleagues were spinning their complex observation theories and marshaling their statistical evidence, a number of individuals with seemingly sensational psychokinetic abilities burst onto the scene. Nevertheless, decades of scientific advances had shattered forever the credibility of the traditional darkened séance room, and any self-proclaimed psychic of the modern age would sooner or later be expected to perform in the bright light of the laboratory.

One of the first of the new psychics to submit to scientific appraisal was Ingo Swann, a Colorado-born artist, writer, and purported astral traveler. In the early 1970s Swann, curious about the then-current idea of affecting plant growth

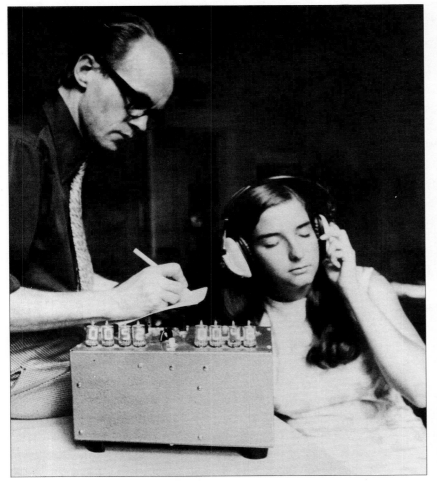

Helmut Schmidt monitors a psychokinesis experiment in which a subject seeks to influence the pattern of clicking sounds emitted by a random number generator. Schmidt invented this device to produce random events, such as clicks or lights, on whose sequence subjects attempt to impose order.

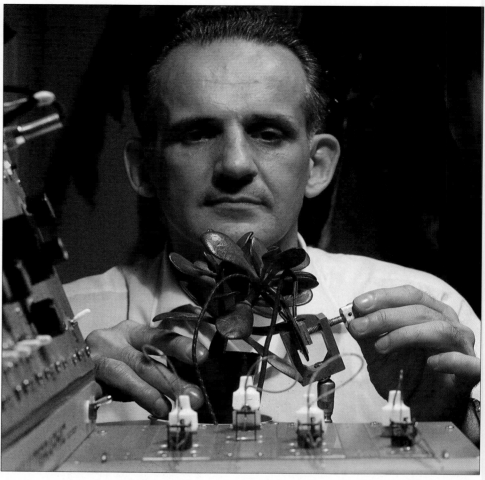

through prayer, purchased a cheap, unhealthy-looking *Dracaena massangeana* and took it to his New York office. At the plant's request, Swann said, he called it Lucifer and talked to it reassuringly. Lucifer responded forcefully, sending mental pictures to make its wants known. Once, overwatered by the office staff in Swann's absence, Lucifer fell into a sorry state. When Swann returned, the wilting plant seemed to demand a sign, Do Not Water. Within a couple of hours after the sign had been posted, Swann reported, Lucifer had perked up, although its soil remained sodden. On another occasion, a droopy Lucifer seemed to be saying something about wanting a penny for its pot. A co-worker with a green thumb cleared up Swann's confusion: Lucifer needed the nutrient copper oxide. Five pennies and a few hours later, the plant had made a full recovery.

October of 1972 found Swann attempting to upset a philodendron by sending it messages about mistreatment, such as having acid poured on its leaves. This plant was in the midtown Manhattan lie-detection school of Cleve Backster, a former CIA interrogations specialist who had become well known in parapsychological circles for using polygraph technology to study the supposed ESP capabilities of plants. Backster had hooked the plant up to a machine that measures changes in electrical resistance. At first, alterations in the plant's electrical resistance corresponded to Swann's threats, but then the responses subsided; Swann concluded that the plant perceived his threats as idle.

Next, Swann persuaded Gertrude R. Schmeidler, a psychology professor at City College in New York, to test his purported ability to change the temperatures of remote objects through PK. The essential equipment included very sensitive thermometers called thermistors and a polygraph device to record temperature changes. In the first experi-

ment, Swann sat facing the polygraph, which would give him instant feedback. The target thermistor was positioned several feet to his left and a control thermistor was strapped to his wrist, to test the possibility that a rise in body heat could affect the target thermistor. With her colleague Larry Lewis as an assistant and observer, Schmeidler gave Swann a series of commands that ran, "Hotter, rest, colder, rest, colder, rest, hotter," and so on. This procedure was designed to eliminate any distortions from progressive or cyclical changes in room temperature. The impossible appeared to come to pass. In seven out of ten series, Schmeidler reported small but significant temperature changes—even when the target thermistors were sealed in vacuum bottles and placed as much as twenty-five feet away from Swann.

During a pause in one experiment, Swann and Schmeidler were in a room adjoining the laboratory suite. Lewis, who had remained in the laboratory, saw the polygraph suddenly register a temperature change. Assuming that someone had unsealed the vacuum bottle, Lewis checked it and found that nothing had been disturbed. But Swann reported that he had begun to wonder about the thermistor's exact location inside the vacuum bottle and had "probed" the interior psychically to find it. He thought that his psychic musing must have inadvertently caused a temperature rise.

From Schmeidler's laboratory Swann went west, to what was then the Stanford Research Institute in Menlo Park, California, to give a demonstration at the invitation of physicist and parapsychologist Harold Puthoff. A harder test than Puthoff devised could scarcely be imagined. He arranged with Stanford University physicist Arthur Hebard to experiment with a highly sensitive magnetometer designed for measuring magnetic fields and detecting quarks, believed to be the smallest units of matter.

Swann's task would be to alter the magnetic field in the magnetometer's core. To accomplish this singular feat, he would have to exert PK through multiple barriers. The magnetometer was encased in an eight-ton iron vault that was set in concrete beneath the laboratory floor; four separate shields, including a supercooled electrical coil, surrounded the core and kept its magnetic field safe from outside influence. Signals from the field were picked up by a small probe and relayed to a chart recorder. If Swann succeeded, any changes in the field would show up in the lines traced by the recorder.

Swann was astounded by the difficulty of the assignment. But he later credited his shock with altering his state of consciousness to a point where he was equal to the herculean task. With Puthoff, the dubious Hebard, and a third physicist, Martin Lee, looking on, Swann set about his supposed mental probing of the magnetometer's core. Suddenly, Puthoff recounted afterward, the steady waves that the chart recorder had been tracing doubled their frequency for half a minute.

The still-skeptical Hebard, whose apparatus was supposedly impenetrable, suggested that something might be wrong with it. Swann would be more convincing, he said, if he could stop the magnetic changes completely. To the amazement of the observers, the wavy lines on the chart recorder flattened out. After about forty-five seconds,

Swann told the men that he could no longer "hold it"; he had to let go. The lines on the chart recorder immediately took on their former undulating pattern, indicating that magnetic activity had resumed.

Puthoff, Hebard, and Lee were stunned. Swann explained that he had peered psychically into the interior of the magnetometer and then made a sketch of what he had seen, including a plate of gold alloy that the physicists had not mentioned to him. As he described the magnetometer, the chart recorder registered still more changes. Puthoff asked Swann not to think about the magnetometer. While they chatted about other matters, the waves remained stable. But when talk once more turned to the apparatus, their frequency increased again. Puthoff could not be completely sure whether Swann had induced a change in the magnetometer itself or merely in the chart recorder. However, Swann's sketch of the magnetometer's interior seemed to provide circumstantial evidence that he had somehow penetrated its defenses, and the three California physicists said they were convinced of his powers. Skeptics hinted broadly that Swann might have used trickery of some sort, but his backers rejected suggestions that he seek to repeat his performance for a group of impartial observers.

Word of the investigations at SRI spread quickly beyond the parapsychology community, and it was not long before Puthoff and Swann found themselves involved in bizarre cloak-and-dagger research for no less a client than the United States government. Their mission was the psychic "viewing" of secret military bases, and although the project was soon terminated for lack of support, its preliminary results did alert the government to the possibility of psychic warfare as a new kind of international threat. One potential weapon in this novel arsenal was the remote viewing of secret military installations and targets by enemy psychics. Another was PK.

Because of the top-secret nature of military intelligence and related activities, it is extremely difficult to determine whether either of the world's superpowers is engaged

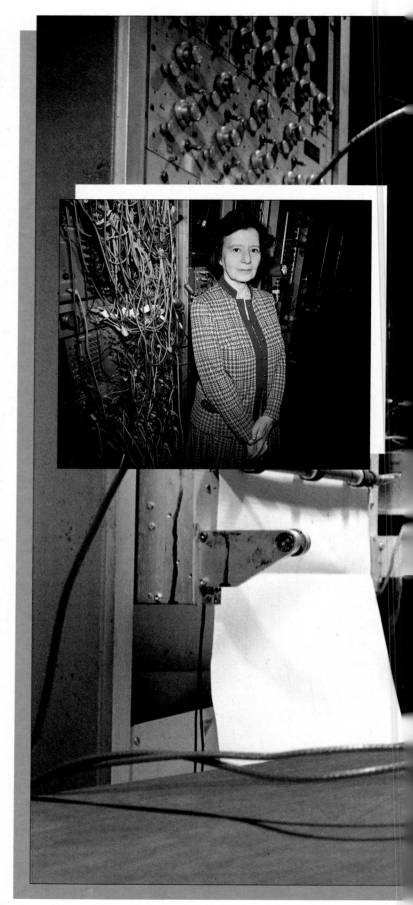

in actual PK weaponry development, much less to assess the quantity and quality of whatever research might be under way. But there is no question that Soviet bloc countries have for years allowed, and perhaps encouraged, the exploration of a relationship between PK, ESP, and the known physical mechanisms and forces.

Scientists studying this conjoining of psi phenomena with engineering call their field "psychotronics," a name that nicely implies both the elusiveness of the mind, or psyche, and the nuts-and-bolts world of science and technology. A clue to one possible line of inquiry in the field appeared in a paper written by Victor G. Adamenko, a physicist and parapsychologist on the staff of Moscow's National Institute of Normal Psychology, and presented at the Second International Congress of Psychotronic Research that met in Monte Carlo in 1975. Adamenko maintained that the brain may possess a psychic energy that it routinely transforms into physicochemical energy, which directly controls the action of the body's muscles. But at times, according to Adamenko, "a rather strong field is being generated which produces an extra-motoric (i.e., with no muscles involved) influence over target objects. That is to say, we are discussing here a quantitative—and not a qualitative—difference in the transformation of the psychical energy into the physico-chemical one." As Adamenko saw it, this influence amounted to a form of psychokinesis.

As to how such a force might be generated or transmitted, and how strong it might be, Adamenko's paper provided no answers. But it did spark speculation that the Soviets might already have made significant progress toward practical applications of psychotronic energy. As Adamenko put it, research in the field might follow at least two different paths. One possibility would be to pursue techniques for improving a psychic's ability to direct psychokinesis or extrasensory perception more accurately at the chosen target. Another objective might be to develop a dual delivery system in which a known type of energy would be used to amplify a psychic's relatively weak output.

Speculation about Soviet progress in the field was fur-

The PK Pretenders

In 1979 two young men offered to test their claimed psychic powers at the McDonnell Laboratory at Washington University. Over the next three years, researchers at the laboratory—which had recently been established with a bequest from aviation pioneer James McDonnell to investigate psychic phenomena—spent about 120 hours and $10,000 working with the pair, and amassed impressive results. The only trouble was that their subjects—Steven Shaw, then eighteen years old, and Michael Edwards, seventeen—were no more than talented magicians. They had insinuated themselves into the experiments at the urging of James Randi, the magician and crusader against the paranormal *(below, center)*.

For years Randi has maintained that psychic research is carried out so casually that hoaxers go undetected. He offers $10,000 to anyone who performs one paranormal feat "under the proper observing conditions."

And researchers have sometimes found to their chagrin that purported psychics may take advantage of poor supervision. At the University of Bath in England, for example, children who had said they could bend metal were caught cheating in 1975 when they were observed through one-way mirrors *(opposite)*.

At McDonnell, Edwards *(below, left)* and Shaw *(below, right)* put on a good show. They bent metal by stroking it, caused a clock to fall off a table, advanced the hands of a watch, and superimposed images on photographs. In fact, as Randi would later disclose, Shaw had previously bent the metal wire that appeared to bow upward under his hand. He edged the clock off a table with a virtually invisible thread stretched between his thumbs. Another clock, a digital model whose readings seemed to

have been turned into gibberish, had been placed in a microwave oven. To create streaks or blotches on photographs, the young men had exposed individual frames of film without removing the roll from the camera. For one series of alleged thoughtographs, in which a psychiatrist discerned parts of a woman's body, Shaw explained, "I spat on the lens."

Not everybody was fooled by the young conjurers; when the videotapes of Shaw's and Edwards's handiwork were presented at a Parapsychological Association meeting in 1981, many in the audience complained about the evident lack of controls. But Randi lost no opportunity to gloat when he announced the hoax at a press conference in early 1983. And a few months later the association formally agreed to invite magicians into experiments to mitigate fraud.

Heralded as "mini-Gellers" for their alleged power to bend metal in the manner of the Israeli mentalist Uri Geller, six children undergoing tests at the University of Bath were caught cheating when they thought they were unobserved. Through a one-way mirror, a camera recorded one child bending a rod underfoot (top) and another covertly using both hands to twist a spoon.

ther fueled by a 1976 report to the Central Intelligence Agency by a California concern called AiResearch Manufacturing Company. According to the report, a Russian expert in radio electronics, Ippolite M. Kogan, may well have spearheaded work on a tandem delivery system to magnify psychic energy when he was director of the Popov Institute's Biocommunication Laboratory in Moscow. Hints of such investigations had trickled out to the West before 1970. In 1975, Kogan's laboratory had been closed down, and his whereabouts were a mystery. But the AiResearch consultants suggested that Soviet scientists would have continued to build on Kogan's intriguing studies of two types of electromagnetic radiation—very low frequency (VLF) and extremely low frequency (ELF) radio waves. The outcome could be an electronic psi-boosting system that, at its most diabolical, could enhance the talents of a gifted psychic to tap into, control, or even destroy human minds.

For a number of reasons, ELF waves have proved to be more interesting to researchers. The longest of all electromagnetic waves, with a span of 1,000 miles between peaks, they follow a path that circles the earth rather than dissipating into space. Michael Persinger, a neuroscientist at Canada's Laurentian University, has speculated that psychics have brain-wave frequencies that coincide with ELF waves and employ them for either receiving or delivering psi effects. More ominously, it has been suggested that ELF waves may be so similar to naturally occurring brain waves that the brain might accept them as its own and be stimulated to imitate the ELF wave patterns. If this is so, a gifted psychic who generated the "strong field" that Adamenko had hypothesized would possess an awesome weapon that could conceivably project brain malfunctions leading to anything from distortions in logical thinking to hallucinations or even death.

All this is highly speculative, of course, as is the very notion that the Soviet Union possesses any ELF-based psychic capability. But the Soviets have already proved to be electromagnetic wizards. In the 1970s, for example, Soviet operatives bombarded the American embassy in Moscow with high levels of microwave radiation—at the other end of the spectrum from ELF waves—reportedly triggering physical and emotional symptoms in the staff. The consensus was that the bombardment was meant either to hinder detection of bugging devices that had been planted in the embassy or to jam American surveillance apparatus. But an imaginative minority of parapsychologists speculated that a telepathic weapon had been directed toward the embassy in an attempt to tune into American brain waves and thus extract information.

Farfetched as it may be, apprehension about Russian psychotronic advances has reached extremes among a handful of mostly retired American military officers. In the mid-1970s, one of them, a retired army officer, Lt. Col.

The mysterious loss of the nuclear submarine Thresher in 1963 was a major disaster. Some paranormalists said the Soviets destroyed the craft through psychotronics—the supposed projection of mental energy so amplified that it becomes a physical or chemical force.

Thomas E. Bearden, helped found a group called the United States Psychotronics Association, which attempted to bring to the government's attention what it perceived as a potentially apocalyptic threat. Bearden believed that psychotronic energy was responsible for a number of unexplained disasters, including the loss of the American nuclear submarine *Thresher* off the coast of Massachusetts in 1963. He asserted that the submarine had been the target in a Soviet experiment with a device that amplified psychotronic energy. The USSR had seven major psychokinetic weapons programs, according to Bearden, who claimed that one of them prompted the serious outbreak of what has come to be known as legionnaires' disease, at an American Legion convention in Philadephia in 1976.

Bearden and his fellow USPA members could muster little more than circumstantial evidence for their claims.

The New York Times.

TEN CENTS

© 1963 by The New York Times Company.
Times Square, New York 36, N. Y.

NEW YORK, THURSDAY, APRIL 11, 1963.

SEATO Reaffirms Support for Laos

By HENRY GINIGER
Special to The New York Times

PARIS, April 10—The eight members of the Southeast Asia Treaty Organization reaffirmed their support today for a neutral and independent Laos in the face of a renewed Communist menace.

In a communiqué capping a two-day meeting, the Council of Ministers of the organization expressed concern over "continued and increased Communist weighting on the neutrality" of the area.

There was no question of intervention of the organization in Laos. As a neutral nation Laos has asked to be no longer a beneficiary of the treaty group's help.

It was strongly hinted, however, that some of SEATO's members would be prepared to make a military stand such as taken in May, 1962, when

Continued on Page 6, Column 3

SOVIET'S CONCERN ON BERLIN GROWS

Moscow Says That NATO's Atomic Program Causes a Special Urgency

By SEYMOUR TOPPING
Special to The New York Times

MOSCOW, April 10—A Soviet

POPE JOHN URGES A WORLD NATION TO GUARD PEACE

His Encyclical on Problems of Atomic Age Proposes Broadening of U.N.

Text of encyclical appears on Pages 17, 18 and 19.

By ARNALDO CORTESI
Special to The New York Times

ROME, April 10—Pope John XXIII proposed in an encyclical today the establishment of a world political community or public authority, a kind of supernation to which all countries should belong. Its aim would be to insure peace.

"The moral order itself," he said, demands that a public authority be established on a worldwide basis.

He made it clear that this new world organization should not be in contrast to or competition with the United Nations, of whose existence the 81-year-old Pontiff took note with satisfaction. He expressed hope that "the day may come when every human being will find therein an effective safeguard for the rights which derive directly from his dignity as a person."

Pope's Eighth Encyclical

The Pope's proposal was contained in an encyclical, or circular letter, dealing with present-

ATOM SUBMARINE WITH 129 LOST IN DEPTHS 220 MILES OFF BOSTON; OIL SLICK SEEN NEAR SITE OF DIVE

Thresher, nuclear-powered attack submarine, commissioned Aug. 3, 1961, at Portsmouth (N. H.) Naval Shipyard

House Votes Works Plan; Backs President, 228-184

By JOHN D. MORRIS
Special to The New York Times

WASHINGTON, April 10—Administration forces won the first major skirmish today in what promises to be a session-long battle over Federal spending. The House of Representatives overrode Republican opposition and approved an appropriation of $450,000,000 for a public works program designed to create jobs in communities with high rates of unemployment.

The roll-call vote was 228 to 184. This affirmed an earlier count of 202 to 172, taken by tellers.

CLAY ADVOCATES FURTHER AID CUT

Declares Additional Savings Won't Be 'Tremendous'—

Lieut. Comdr. John Wesley Harvey, skipper of craft.

United Press International

Thresher reported down in the Atlantic at cross.

The New York Times April 11, 1963

THRESHER HUNTED

Rescue Craft Search Area of Last Test in 8,400-Foot Water

By ROBERT F. WHITNEY
Special to The New York Times

WASHINGTON, April 10—The Navy said tonight that its atomic submarine Thresher and 129 men aboard "appeared to be lost" in the Atlantic.

An oil slick was reported to have been sighted in the area where the vessel took a deep test dive at about 9 o'clock this morning in water 8,400 feet deep, 220 miles east of Boston.

"At that depth," said Adm. George W. Anderson, Chief of Naval Operations, "rescue would be absolutely out of the question."

Loss of the Thresher and 129 men would be the Navy's worst peacetime submarine disaster.

However, the Navy still clung to the possibility that there had been a communications failure and the $45,000,000 submarine was unable to report by radio or otherwise.

Revival of Saloons,

KENNEDY WEIGHS

Even so, at least a few members of the military establishment seem to have hearkened to their warnings. For example, the authors of a U.S. Army study that was partly declassified in 1981 stressed the importance of remaining open-minded about psychokinesis, which they described as a form of energy that could have significant military applications. The Soviet Union, they wrote, "appears to have made significant progress toward developing psychotronic weapons." They defined psychotronics as "the projection or transmission of mental energy by individual or collective mental discipline and control, or by an energy-emitting device—a kind of mind jammer." The report stated unequivocally that "the technology, physics and mathematics involved are real, and not matters of the occult or supernatural. Details of psychotronics offer a 'physics of metaphysics'—a fully developed theory of paranormal phenomena that unites physics and psychology."

Army reports, of course, can fall into error, but one country cannot dismiss out of hand the possibility that another military power is experimenting with a radically different type of weaponry. As recently as 1987, the U.S. Army examined the merits of psychokinesis as a means of jamming enemy computers, triggering nuclear weapons, or incapacitating weapons and vehicles.

The study did not, however, find persuasive evidence for the existence of psi phenomena. Indeed, for all the apparent advances in laboratory techniques that PK researchers have made since J. B. Rhine's early dice-throwing experiments, their goal remains elusive. They have yet to produce experimental results that are repeatable, that will persuade skeptics that psi is a reality.

Still hopeful, some researchers have been rethinking the conventional distinctions that have been made among psi processes. PK, they suggest, has often been confused with the phenomenon of precognition. For example, a new look at hundreds of random number generator experiments carried out between 1969 and 1984 prompted a team of parapsychologists and statisticians at the University of California and SRI International—as the former Stanford Research Institute is now called—to propose a whole new hypothesis. It may well be, they say, that subjects, instead of causing a set of results by exerting PK, somehow extract knowledge from the experimental process, enabling them to guess in advance what the results will be.

Such intuitive data sorting—a term these researchers use instead of precognition—does away with a very knotty problem raised whenever a change is attributed to PK. For after many decades of laboratory investigation, PK remains a mystery. If it exists, if it can indeed cause physical changes—in radioactive material, computers, people, or any other target—it must be, from a scientific point of view, a physical force comparable to gravity, electromagnetism, or the special forces governing nuclear particles. Nevertheless, the fact remains that no one has ever produced any evidence that PK is another natural force. And, despite much research, none of the forces already known has been proven to account for PK. Some parapsychologists join J. B. Rhine in the belief that it is a mistake to treat psychokinesis as a physical force. They firmly maintain that it is an aspect of will, of soul, of consciousness, and that it is not bound by any of the physical laws.

ith such diametrically opposed views coming into play, it is difficult to imagine what common theoretical ground quantum physicists, parapsychologists, psychotronic warriors, and spiritualists will ever be able to find. But while theorists search, quibble, and argue, the more pragmatistic are eager to make use of the supposed force of psychokinesis, no matter what its nature and mechanics may be. And if it is truly an operative phenomenon, the implications—from medical uses to agriculture to psychic warfare—would be staggering. Some researchers propose that biological application of PK could lead to a control over heredity and even evolution. Others dream more modestly of a foolproof gambling system or financial scheme, or a sports team that wins every game. In fact, it is doubtful that anyone—even the most dedicated skeptic—would turn down a chance to master the secrets of true psychokinesis.

Seeking the Sources of PK

Possibly the most daunting challenge that faces modern psi researchers is to explain what force—or forces—could be responsible for the strange phenomena attributed to psychokinesis, or PK. Quite simply, the notion that tangible objects might change their form or location with no apparent application of physical force is all but impossible for conventional physics to accept.

But many PK enthusiasts point to a more easily grasped concept: the idea that it is possible, in varying degrees, for the human brain to interact directly with its environment. Perhaps, some speculate, certain psychically gifted people can modulate their brain waves to achieve control over events in the physical world. As evidence, parapsychologists offer laboratory experiments that seemingly associate certain types of brain waves with PK and other allegedly psychic occurrences. The four major types of brain waves, as measured and charted by an electroencephalograph, are shown below, with descriptions of the activities usually linked with each.

In their efforts to establish a theoretical basis for PK, parapsychologists turn also to certain modern scientific principles that appear to suggest models for paranormal physical occurrences. To some psychic researchers, for example, the strange, unpredictable behavior of subatomic particles seems to be similar to certain PK effects. Others say that PK may be attributed to invisible energy contained in these particles or perhaps in such phenomena as heat and sound. The theories of these psi investigators are illustrated on the following six pages. No parapsychologist, however, has yet satisfactorily explained how the human mind might interact with such forces, thus shaping physical events.

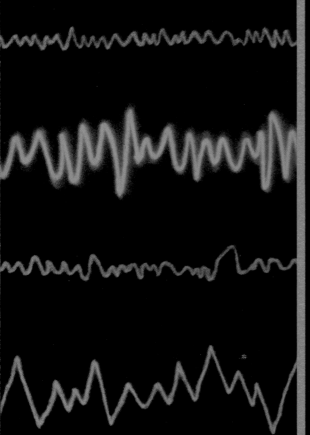

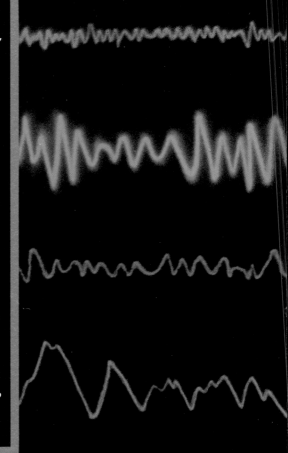

BETA. *The small, close peaks of beta waves are most often charted when a person is awake and alert. Walking, talking, dialing a telephone, and reading a book are all activities that require beta-type brain activity. During periods of anxiety or intense concentration, the brain may remain in the beta mode, even when the eyes are closed.*

ALPHA. *This is the state of mind that some PK researchers suggest is associated with PK effects. Each time a person closes his or her eyes, the brain generates a burst of alpha waves, but it is the longer, sustained periods of alpha that signify the alert, relaxed mood in which a person is highly receptive to outside signals. This state can be induced through hypnosis, meditation, listening to music, and even by watching television.*

THETA. *In adults, theta waves usually denote a deep trance, a mode that some mystics can enter at will. When theta waves dominate, sensations of pain may be dulled; thus, a yogi or fakir whose brain is putting forth theta waves may be able to lie comfortably on a bed of nails or endure piercing wounds without wincing.*

DELTA. *Delta waves, with their stretched-out peaks, are slower than most other waves and are usually generated during sleep. Some neuroscientists believe that delta waves are also a defense mechanism: When the brain is endangered by injury or disease, it may lapse into delta-wave emission.*

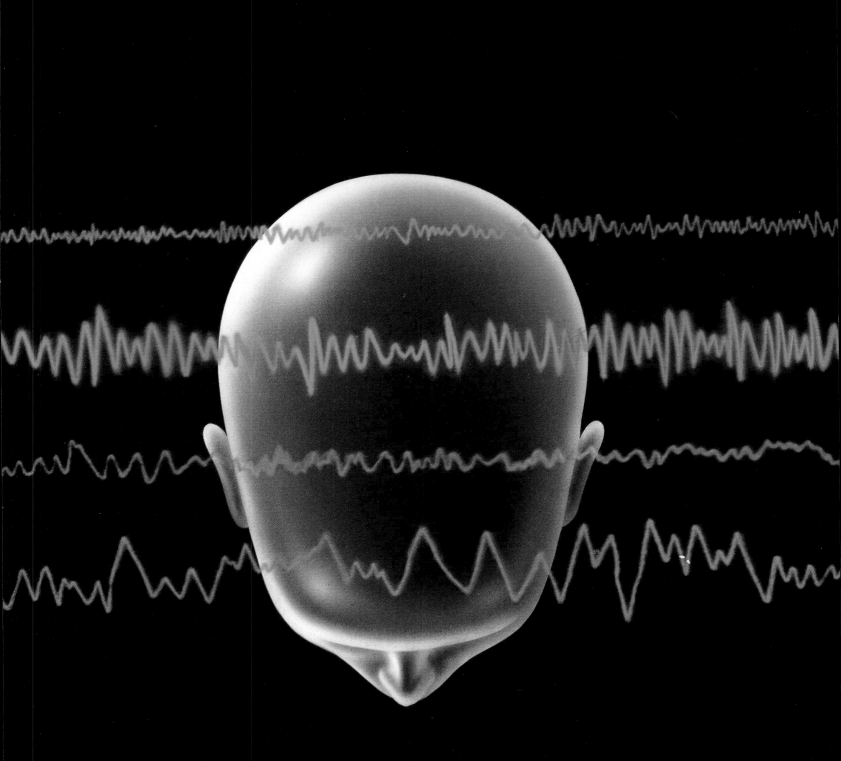

Quantum Comparisons

Some parapsychologists have turned to the perplexing principles of quantum mechanics in hopes of explaining how mind might affect matter. In the microworld of subatomic particles, events are often unpredictable—and no less bizarre, perhaps, than a teacup passing unscathed through a solid barrier *(left)*.

A few PK researchers, notably the German-born physicist Helmut Schmidt, claim to have demonstrated that psychically gifted observers can affect events at the quantum level *(pages 71-72)*. And some parapsychologists reason that if this power exists, it might be brought to bear on the macroworld as well.

Take, for example, the notion that a cup could pass through a barrier. By the laws of everyday science, such an incident seems impossible. How can one solid object pass through another? Yet some psychics claim the ability to make an object disappear from one location and reappear in another. This so-called teleportation is sometimes said to enable someone to move items from room to room, or from inside to outside a container.

As it happens, microparticles behave in somewhat similar fashion, tunneling through barriers and showing up in places that classical physics decrees they should not be. Yet even an item such as a cup is made up of innumerable microparticles. If these tiny units can permeate barriers, ask some psi researchers, might it not be possible under certain circumstances for the entire cup to pass from one side of a wall to the other? Fascinating though this analogy may be, however, mainstream scientists generally assert that the laws of the microworld cannot be applied directly to the larger macroworld.

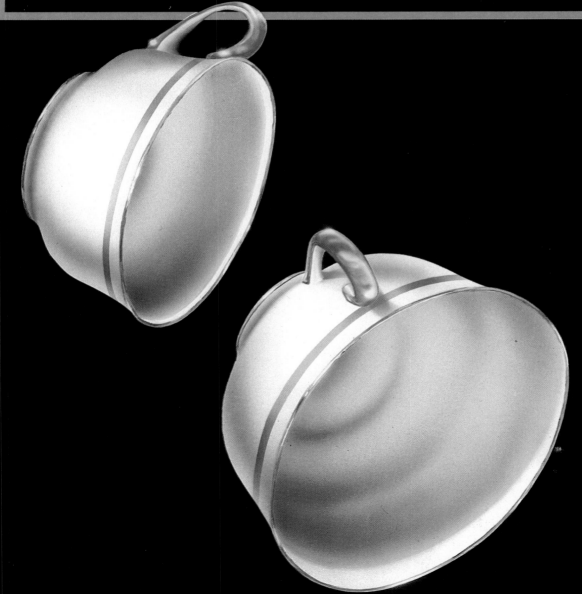

Surfaces of Action

In the mid-1970s, John Hasted, an English physicist, became fascinated with the alleged feats of psychics who claimed the ability to bend such articles as keys and spoons without applying physical force. Seeking an explanation, he launched a series of experiments with children who were supposedly able to deform metal without touching it.

Hasted concerned himself primarily with small, scarcely discernible changes, rather than with dramatic effects such as twisted spoons. Placing door keys in several locations in a room and stationing one of his test subjects nearby, he used sensitive gauges attached to the keys in order to determine whether some force had been exerted upon the metal. During numerous sessions, Hasted reported, delicate variations in pressure were indeed registered. When a child was not nearby, he said, there were no apparent signs of strain on the door keys.

Hasted went on to work out a novel theory explaining how this phenomenon could occur, particularly when the children were several feet from their target objects. Complicating his task was the fact that keys positioned in several places around a room sometimes seemed to register stress simultaneously. Perhaps, Hasted reasoned, force waves were somehow emanating from each child's body. Based on his precise positioning of the keys, Hasted speculated that these waves were shaped like planes or slabs—"surfaces of action."

At times, according to Hasted, the plane might actually twist, in the manner of the band extending from the hand shown below. This twisting activity, he thought, could cause a spoon or other metal object to form a series of bends.

Interestingly, Hasted said he was able to measure and record evidence of the phenomenon more frequently when his subjects were in a relaxed, almost inattentive state of mind, a mood associated with alpha brain waves. When the children concentrated too hard, they were generally unable to produce the purported surface of action and the resultant strain on the keys.

Energies of Levitation

A basic law of physics dictates that no object can be moved without an expenditure of energy. If a table is levitated, for example, some force must be present, causing it to rise into the air *(below)*. But where could such a force come from? And how could a person tap into this energy and direct it in order to effect psychokinesis?

Parapsychologists have attempted to answer these questions throughout this century. In one early series of experiments, a psi researcher maintained that everyone present during sessions in which a table seemed to levitate had lost a few ounces of weight. He took this as an indication that all of those in the group had somehow contributed a small amount of their own energy to the apparent PK.

More recently, PK enthusiasts have speculated that heat, or possibly sound, might supply the necessary force. According to one researcher, cooling the temperature in a room by a single degree Celsius would release enough energy to lift an armchair several hundred feet into the air. As for the supposition that sound can generate PK energy, there are those who suggest that this might account for the music some psychics play in order to facilitate their alleged powers. In either case, some psi researchers speculate, sound or heat waves might coalesce into a form of coherent energy, which could then be directed at an object. The process could be similar, they say, to the way a laser beam acquires its power by concentrating and directing light.

A basic question still remains: What could cause essentially diffuse energy to converge? Not surprisingly, one proposed answer points again to a possible power of the human mind over matter. Perhaps, psi researchers conjecture, specially gifted people possess the ability to use will—or consciousness—to seize inchoate energy and to consolidate it into a force that is capable of moving objects at their bidding.

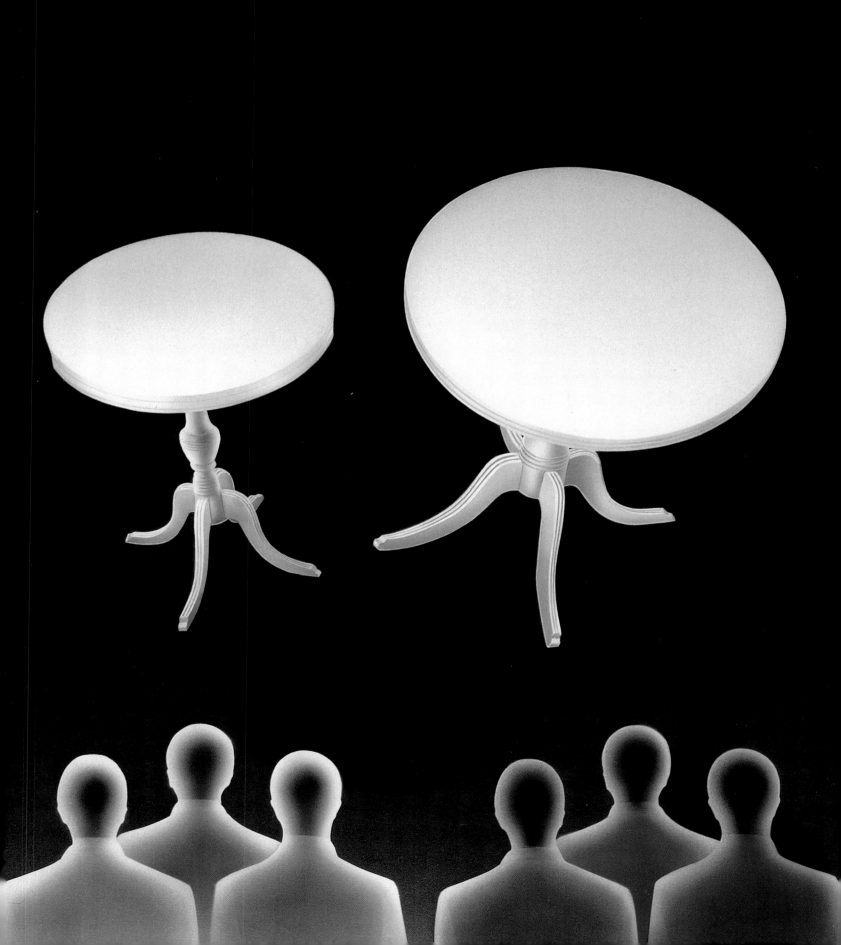

The Hypnotic State

For almost as long as humans have sought relief from suffering or answers to prayers, they have turned for help to a sleeplike state now known as hypnosis. The priests of ancient Greece and Egypt put people into trances to treat their physical or mental troubles; the salons of eighteenth-century Europe dabbled in an unseen but potent "animal magnetism" that convulsed and then purportedly cured its subjects. Yet to this day, hypnosis, a condition in which the subconscious seems to hold sway over the conscious mind, is not fully understood.

The modern history of hypnosis begins with Franz Anton Mesmer, an Austrian physician of the 1700s who believed he was channeling an invisible magnetic force that healed the sick. Mesmer gave his name to the phenomenon, mesmerism, but later practitioners dismissed his theory of magnetism, saying that the hypnotist himself somehow controlled the subject. Later still, the focus shifted again: It was only through the subject's willingness, or suggestibility, that the hypnotist acquired his seeming mastery. Today, many believe that hypnosis represents an altered state of consciousness; some scientists, however, suspect that subjects are merely role playing, albeit unconsciously, to please the hypnotist.

Whatever the explanation, hypnosis has been turned to a number of uses—to block pain, to provide entertainment, to summon up long-suppressed memories or emotions, to improve skill at a sport or a performing art. Even if hypnosis is only a means for subjects to do what they want, the results suggest the power of the mind over the limits of matter.

A mesmerist induces a hypnotic state in a woman.
As this eighteenth-century engraving shows, some mesmerists believed
they could channel magnetic force through their hands.

Mesmer's Fabulous Magnets

Though called the father of hypnotism, Franz Anton Mesmer never really understood the phenomenon he made famous. Mesmer, born in 1734 and trained as a physician, believed that all matter was suspended in an invisible magnetic fluid over which the planets and stars exerted a gravitational pull. When the fluid became imbalanced in people, they fell sick. The remedy was to pass magnets over their bodies. They then went into what Mesmer called a "beneficial crisis," often accompanied by convulsions, and were pronounced cured.

Starting in the 1770s, in Vienna and Paris, Mesmer passed his magnet over much of the fashionable world, particularly its women. To accommodate them all, he built a *baquet,* a large covered tub around which thirty people could be magnetized at once. It held ground glass, iron filings, and bottles of so-called magnetized water. Patients grasped iron rods that protruded from the baquet and applied them to afflicted parts of their bodies. As hidden musicians played softly—Mesmer was a patron of the

young Mozart—Mesmer would enter in a purple robe, often playing a glass harmonica and waving an iron wand.

The scientific establishment roundly dismissed Mesmer and his magnets. In 1784, a royal commission of nine scientists headed by Benjamin Franklin, then the American ambassador to France, investigated Mesmer's technique and called it fraudulent. Patients responded only if they

knew they were being magnetized, the commission said; hence, "magnetism" was merely the patients' belief and imagination and could not be curative.

Ironically, the commission understood the nature of hypnosis better than Mesmer, who insisted that it had a physiological basis. And the verdict destroyed Mesmer. Disgraced, he left for Switzerland, where he died penniless in 1815.

Franz Mesmer (above) and his views are satirized in this 1784 engraving, in which a mesmerist stands on a globe to channel magnetism from the heavens. The hot-air balloon, a recent invention, had furthered popular belief in the power of invisible forces such as magnetism.

In this engraving of Mesmer's Paris salon, the wealthy sit around a baquet while a woman swoons; in a room at the rear, the poor are treated for free. The salon was hung with mirrors, supposedly to intensify the magnetic force.

A contemporary caricature portrays the mesmerist as an ass, a figure often used to symbolize quackery. In the background, two patients are shown as sheep.

The Doctors' Dispute

Mesmer's departure from the scene opened the door for a more thoughtful exploration of hypnosis in the 1800s, and for the recognition that it is a psychological rather than a physiological phenomenon.

A French nobleman, the Marquis de Puységur, took the first step in that direction. A pupil of Mesmer, de Puységur hypnotized peasants on his estate. He observed that subjects, though in a deep trance, responded readily to suggestions, and he found that they afterward frequently possessed no recollection of events—a condition that has come to be known as posthypnotic amnesia.

While de Puységur continued to believe in magnetism, one of his pupils, a Portuguese priest named José Custodio di Faria, argued that hypnosis was a kind of lucid sleep that involved nothing more

than the acquiescence of the subject. A few decades later James Braid, a British surgeon, determined that a subject could be put into a trance by concentrating on a single idea. It was Braid who coined the familiar word *hypnosis* from Hypnos, the Greek god of sleep.

Those ideas would be developed further in France, by a physician who lived near the city of Nancy. In the 1860s, Dr. Ambroise August Liébeault offered his patients a choice: conventional medicine, for a fee, or treatment by hypnosis, without charge. When his hypnotic cure worked on a sciatica patient who had been treated unsuccessfully by Hippolyte Bernheim, a professor of medicine at the University of Nancy, the highly respected Bernheim began to collaborate with Liébeault. Ultimately the two treated more

than 12,000 patients at their hypnosis clinic, which also attracted such significant visitors as the pioneering psychologist Sigmund Freud. But Freud, reportedly an inept hypnotist, found results with his patients too transitory and soon dropped the technique in favor of psychoanalysis.

As the century waned, the old physiological view of hypnosis was championed a final time. Jean-Martin Charcot, an eminent neurologist at the Salpêtrière Hospital in Paris, found that hysterical symptoms could be both produced and relieved by hypnosis, and he declared that hypnosis was a physiological condition that would work only for hysterics. Before he died in 1893, Charcot conceded that he had been wrong; even so, his research helped to make hypnotism a legitimate field of inquiry in the medical community.

Dr. Ambroise Liébeault, who used hypnosis in his clinic in France, stands at left with staff and patients in this 1900 photograph.

British surgeon James Braid's research reinforced the emerging view of hypnosis as a psychological phenomenon.

In a hypnotic trance, a young peasant named Victor Race obeys the Marquis de Puységur's suggestion to lap milk like a cat. A particularly apt subject, Race believed hypnosis helped relieve an inflammation of his lung.

French neurologist Jean-Martin Charcot demonstrates to colleagues the effects of hypnosis on one of his hysterical patients.

Hypnotism Goes on Stage

Long before the scientific community began to take hypnosis seriously, the public had embraced it as a form of entertainment. Beginning in the early nineteenth century, stage hypnotists flourished, and home hypnosis became a popular parlor game. Some reports have it that enthusiasts included novelist Charles Dickens, who is said to have excelled at inducing trances.

Unfortunately for serious practitioners, the rise of hypnosis led to a number of false impressions about its powers—many of which survive today. Then as now, stage hypnotists were only too happy to claim that they could make people act totally out of character. "You can make a Democrat make a Republican speech, or make a Republican make a Democratic speech," asserted one Professor T. C. Cole, Jr., in his 1900 mail-order course in hypnotism. "You can have them riding brooms for horses, fishing with a broom for a fishing pole." (The professor admitted, however, that he always took along a few of his own seasoned hypnotic subjects when he performed in public, just in case.)

Such a view of a hypnotist's powers had its thrillingly sinister side, and this aspect was fully exploited by novelists and moviemakers. Hypnotism was frequently portrayed in their works as a force for evil, exercised by manipulative villains who placed their victims in trances, then ordered them to awake and carry out deviously concocted plans. The epitome of the powerful fictional hypnotist was Svengali, who made his appearance in the 1894 novel *Trilby*, by English author George Du Maurier. To make himself a fortune, Svengali hypnotized the beautiful but untalented heroine to become a famous singer.

Under hypnosis, three suggestible instrumentalists play make-believe music with some common household items.

A stage hypnotist named Handy-Bandy transfixes his assistant, a woman with the equally colorful name of Nadia-Nadyr, in this 1927 poster from Germany. Exotic dress enhanced the hypnotist's image as someone with mysterious powers.

The evil Dr. Caligari, having hypnotized a man to carry out his vile schemes, displays the zombie-like subject to the terrified heroine in this still from the 1919 German film classic The Cabinet of Dr. Caligari. The mad doctor keeps the mesmerized wretch in his cabinet, releasing him only to murder innocent townsfolk.

In a stunt put on by generations of stage hypnotists, a woman lies suspended between two chairs. In fact, most people can perform the same feat without benefit of hypnosis—although they should take care to avoid neck injuries.

Unlocking Memory

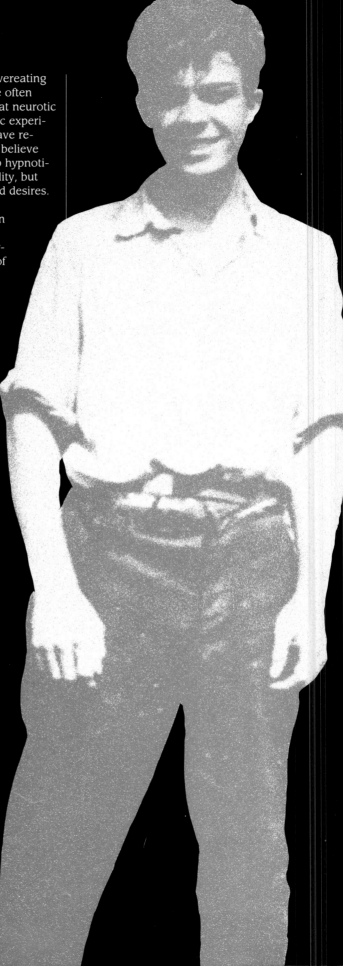

It was not until the early 1900s that hypnosis began to win the respect of the scientific community. Today it is used in the treatment of pain, in psychotherapy, and even in law enforcement.

That hypnosis has become a tool in psychotherapy is due largely to the efforts of Milton Erickson, a Wisconsin farmer's son born in 1901. Totally paralyzed by polio at the age of seventeen, Erickson was strapped upright in a rocking chair one day, wishing he were nearer the window, when he noticed that, almost imperceptibly, the chair had begun to rock. Had his longing somehow made his body move? In the following months, he practiced a form of self-hypnosis as he worked at regaining the power of movement. His technique was to search his memory for the sensation of a movement, such as grasping a pitchfork; he would then stare at his hand until his fingers began to twitch. Gradually the movements became stronger and within his conscious control. Less than a year after he first made his chair rock, Erickson was up on crutches, and in time he would walk unaided, with only a slight limp.

Erickson went on to become a psychiatrist, and he was among the first to apply hypnosis to psychotherapy. It is now widely used in behavior modification, for such problems as smoking or overeating —although beneficial results are often short-lived. It is also used to treat neurotic patients by uncovering traumatic experiences and thoughts they may have repressed. But many psychiatrists believe that recollections summoned up hypnotically may reflect not a strict reality, but the patient's fantasies, fears, and desires.

When it comes to criminal investigations, hypnosis is an even more controversial issue. While there are cases of witnesses correctly recalling obscure details of a crime after being hypnotized, such subjects have been shown to be easily swayed by hypnotic suggestion—and thus highly unreliable. Nonetheless, the Supreme Court ruled in 1987 that defendants may introduce as evidence remarks they made under hypnosis.

Hypnosis has been better accepted as a means of controlling pain; indeed, in 1958 the American Medical Association endorsed its use for this purpose. It is being used today to control pain in burn victims, cancer patients, and women in childbirth.

Milton Erickson, shown here with his daughter-in-law Lillian, pioneered the use of hypnosis in psychiatry. Many therapists prefer it to Freudian psychoanalysis to treat nervous symptoms.

In 1919, a young Milton Erickson stands unsupported after overcoming paralysis (left). In addition to drawing on memory to restore movement, Erickson said, he also relied on observation, watching his baby sister struggling to walk and consciously retraining his own body to do the same.

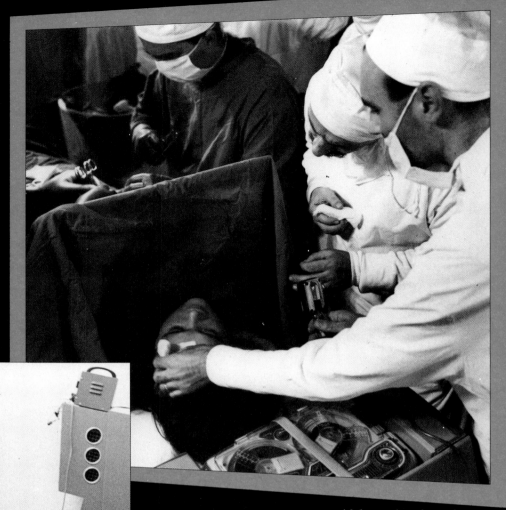

With hypnosis as her only anesthetic, a nineteen-year-old Italian girl undergoes an appendectomy in 1961. Because hypnosis does not depress breathing or circulation, it is a desirable anesthetic, but not everyone can be put into a trance deep enough for major surgery.

Her hand immersed in ice water, a hypnosis subject in an experiment at Stanford University reports no pain. Studies show that subjects experience pain on some level but that it does not register on their consciousness.

During the years since Mesmer's magnets, the method of inducing a hypnotic state in a subject has been greatly simplified and demystified. Today it is generally recognized that the critical task for the hypnotist is to win the trust and cooperation of the subject. Once rapport has been established, the hypnotist can use any of a large number of induction techniques.

Whatever the specific procedure, most subjects are told to concentrate on and listen to the hypnotist, to relax, to close their eyes, and to try to imagine what is being suggested. Hypnotists frequently ask their subjects to focus on an object, with the goal of having them close their eyes; the object should be above eye level so that staring will be tiring and the eyelids will droop.

Often, this method is combined with a procedure called progressive relaxation, in which the subject is urged to relax each muscle in the body. The hypnotist drones on, suggesting that "waves of relaxation" are repeatedly washing over the subject, that he is becoming drowsy and can no longer keep his eyes open voluntarily— but that at the same time the subject is choosing to close them.

There are a number of variations on the theme. As an alternative relaxation technique, some subjects are told to clench one fist, let all their tension flow into it, and then unclench to let the tension escape. Others are instructed to count backward by ones or by threes or to count the cycle of their breaths, all the while concentrating on the hypnotist's patter. Another common procedure involves movement—such as touching palms, lifting an arm in the air, dropping an arm—in response to the hypnotist's suggestion.

More sophisticated are the so-called imaging methods, in which subjects are invited to imagine a scene and, figuratively speaking, to enter it. The scene may be inviting, such as a beach, a cloud, or a sunrise. Or subjects may be told to imagine themselves on a staircase, escalator, or elevator, with each downward step or stage taking them into a deeper hypnotic state.

In such cases, the hypnotic trance can be terminated by reversing the procedure; subjects imagine themselves walking up the staircase, for example. In general, though, trances are terminated very simply; the hypnotist either tells the subject directly to wake up or counts backward from ten—or sometimes twenty—to one while the subject gradually awakens.

Most people can be hypnotized, although the degree of their suggestibility can vary greatly. This level of receptivity can be tested in a number of ways. A patient who has raised an arm at the hypnotist's suggestion may, without apparent effort, hold it in the air for an hour or more. Positive and negative hallucinations are another measure: A loud noise may go unheard because the hypnotist says it will, while an imaginary noise is heard—and may be stopped, at the hypnotist's suggestion, with a single gesture by the subject. Or the hypnotist may even ask subjects to evaluate the depth of a trance by ranking it on a numerical scale.

Hypnotist Harvey Misel (right) guides Chicago White Sox outfielder Ron Kittle into a trance in 1983. Kittle hit thirty-five home runs that year, but there is no proof that hypnotism helped.

A subject is hypnotized by watching a swinging pendulum. Known as the Chevreul pendulum, after the nineteenth-century Frenchman who popularized it, the device has become synonymous with hypnotism; in fact, it is rarely used now as an induction procedure.

Do-It-Yourself Hypnosis

Many experts in the field maintain that most people are capable of hypnotizing themselves as a means of reducing stress or alleviating pain. One simple method, according to psychologist Stanley N. Chase, involves making a tape recording of the following instructions. The recording can be played back at any time as an aid to self-hypnosis:

Sit in a comfortable chair with your back supported, feet on the floor, and hands in your lap. Then take a few deep, slow breaths as you begin to relax, relaxing especially your arms and shoulders. Make your arms feel very heavy as you breathe deeply and regularly.

Now, breathing normally and continuing to relax, stare straight ahead. Keeping your head level, raise only your eyes to a point on the ceiling or high on the wall. You may choose an imaginary spot in the middle of a blank area. Continue to stare at the spot for thirty to sixty seconds or until your eyes feel as if they want to close. There may be a slight strain on your eyes, they may get blurry or watery, but continue to stare. Keeping your eyes raised, slowly lower your eyelids until they are closed. Let your head fall forward comfortably, and relax. Relax more deeply.

Begin counting very slowly from one to five, breathing out slowly as you say each number to yourself. With each number, you are drifting more deeply into a relaxed state. You feel the relaxation flow down through your body.

When you reach five, pause, and count again very slowly, relaxing even more deeply. Repeat these sets of five as long as you continue to feel more and more relaxed with each set.

After these sets of five, gradually begin to get rid of distracting thoughts as they enter your mind, and drift deeper into relaxation. You are wiping away any distracting thoughts and drifting more deeply into a relaxed state. To relax more deeply, you may choose to imagine a relaxing scene, like a beach or a mountain lake; perhaps you are observing it, perhaps you are in the scene.

You can end your self-hypnosis at any point, says Chase. Simply count backward, slowly, from five to one, and open your eyes after reaching one.

CHAPTER 3

Mind over Body

he incongruous setting for the ceremony is the grounds of a hotel in southern California; the improbable hour is 1:00 a.m. About a hundred people, nearly all of them strangers to one another, have gathered on the greensward near the parking lot in hopes of performing a small miracle of the human spirit. It is their intention to walk on fire.

Their leader and instructor in this enterprise is a handsome, garrulous man in his late twenties who stands before them at the head of a pair of parallel beds of sod filled with blazing hardwood coals. Each bed is ten feet long and three feet wide. Sparks swirl into the damp night air as the embers pop and rumble; the people, too, are charged, noisy. As they form two lines—one in front of each glowing sod bed—most of them are, as instructed, muttering a calming phrase: "cool moss, cool moss." They are barefoot.

All eyes on him, the leader huffs several noisy breaths and steps resolutely onto one of the blankets of fire. Three, four, five swift strides and he emerges onto the lawn to wipe the cinders from his feet. The men and women in the rapt crowd erupt in cheers. They feel a surge of faith and confidence; their qualms have been all but banished, and they are eager to fulfill their potential, as their leader has promised they would. "What are you going to do when you have achieved success?" he has asked them—and then answered his own question: "You're going to celebrate!"

And celebrate they do, whooping and waving their fists triumphantly, as one by one they tread the path of fire. Nearly all of them make the crossing; none are burned; few are even blistered. From each one, the leader, who is also a businessman, has collected $145. The fee covers not only the stroll over now-orange coals, but also the four-hour inspirational seminar that preceded it. During this lecture, the leader, Tony Robbins of Los Angeles, explains that in the few seconds a person needs to confront and walk the fiery trench, his life will be transformed. Once people find the will to take that first step, Robbins tells the students, they discover the secret to success, health, and contentment. Grand claims, without a doubt—but satisfied customers are not hard to find. "It turned my life around," reports an elderly woman of Robbins's teachings. "It's something greater than confidence; it's reassurance that anything is possible."

Once the human mind is properly prepared, anything *is* possible—that is Robbins's tantalizing message. And he is only one preacher of that hopeful gospel. Fire walking, with its inherent drama and its links to humankind's primitive past, has attracted not a few latter-day gurus and disciples. But the notion that the mind's power is capable of being harnessed in the service of self-improvement underlies a wide array of practices and schools of thought. These range from such exotic feats as levitation—rising into the air by seemingly paranormal means—to the homespun dictums of *The Power of Positive Thinking,* that durable paean to optimism written in 1952 by the ebullient Dr. Norman Vincent Peale.

Those who extol the benefits of such mind-over-body techniques as biofeedback or creative visualization may scoff at the entrepreneurial evangelists of fire walking, which one writer sardonically dismissed as "the ultimate one-stop, cut-rate, cosmic self-improvement seminar." But it seems clear that Tony Robbins, with his intensity and his watchwords, "cool moss, cool moss," has imparted a measure of resolve to some people. One believer, a college professor, declared that Robbins helped him conquer a fear of flying. "The other day a friend invited me to go on a small plane," he said, "and I started to get queasy when we were going over the mountains. I immediately visualized the fire walk. I just cool mossed myself, and that did it."

Fire walking as therapy is a relatively recent notion. But as a religious and magical ritual, it is too ancient to trace and curiously widespread. By about 500 BC, it was firmly established in China, Japan, Tibet, and India. Over the years it spread westward to the Mediterranean region and Europe.

In medieval times, people walked on fire to show their humility or to seek purification and divine blessing. Others did so to prove their innocence of such crimes as murder or heresy. Those who were blameless, it was thought, would escape injury after crossing red-hot coals. Similar applications persisted into the modern age, especially in technologically primitive cultures.

One of the first westerners to give an account of a ritual fire walk was Dr. William Tufts Brigham, director of the Bishop Museum of Ethnology in Honolulu. In the 1880s, Brigham, who had grown up in Hawaii, persuaded three kahunas, or native priests, to introduce him to the ways of fire walking. He chose an opportune time: A volcanic eruption near the huge active crater of Kilauea had just brought forth a fresh flow of lava.

After an arduous three-day climb, they reached the source of the flow. "It was a grand sight," Brigham recalled. "The side of the mountain had broken open just above the timber line and the lava was spouting out of several vents—shooting with a roar as high as 200 feet, and falling to make a great bubbling pool." Following a stream of boiling overflow, they found a level strip the kahunas considered ideal for their purpose. Brigham, however, was having his regrets. The lava path was more than 100 feet long; heat rose from it in pulsating, shimmering waves. Even at a distance, he wrote, "it was far worse than a bake oven . . . the lava was blackening on the surface, but all across it ran heat discolorations that came and went as they do on a cooling iron before a blacksmith plunges it into his tub for tempering. I heartily wished that I had not been so curious."

While Brigham summoned his nerve, his companions unstrapped their sandals and wrapped their feet with leaves, as is traditional. Brigham, to the great amusement of the three priests, chose sturdier armor—hobnailed boots with thick leather soles, and two pairs of socks.

The moment, both sought for and dreaded by Brigham, had come. Together, the priests droned a brief, solemn prayer. "I was almost roasted alive before the kahunas had finished their chanting," Brigham wrote, "although it could not have taken more than a few minutes." It was decided that the oldest kahuna would go first and that Brigham would follow.

"Without a moment of hesitation the oldest man trotted out on that terrifically hot surface," the ethnologist remembered. "I was watching him with my mouth open and he was nearly across—a distance of about 150 feet—when someone gave me a shove that resulted in my having a choice of falling on my face on the lava or catching a running stride."

Brigham ran, boots and all. It took only a few steps for the soles of his boots to curl and shrink: Quickly their seams burst, and then he was running in burning socks. His face and body felt as though he were standing inside a furnace—but in his feet, he remarked later, there was virtually no sensation. Reaching at last the end of the fiery trough, Brigham leaped to safety and stamped out the fire in his socks. His boots, left far behind, had turned to ash, but there was not a blister on his feet or even a feeling of warmth. Nor did any of the kahunas suffer injury, though the cocoons of leaves about their feet had burned away completely.

A swift runner as a young man, Dr. William Tufts Brigham (below) recalled that he must have "broken all records" when he dashed unhurt across molten lava on the flank of Hawaii's Mt. Kilauea in the late 1880s. The volcano remains active, as the recent eruption shows.

Brigham lived for some forty years more, yet this man of science could never fathom the stunt he had achieved. "It's magic," was his meek conclusion, "part of the magic done by the kahunas and other primitive peoples."

In 1922 the Roman Catholic bishop of Mysore, India, attended a fire walk at the palace of the local maharajah. To the bishop's alarm, the Muslim mystic who led the event started off by pushing an unsuspecting palace servant into the glowing bed of coals. For a few horrifying moments, the servant struggled desperately to escape. Then, wrote the bishop, "the look of terror on his face gave place to an astonished smile, and he proceeded to cross the trench lengthwise, beaming contentedly on those who were standing round on either side of him."

As if this demonstration were not stunning enough, the maharajah's entire orchestra then marched into the glowing embers. Nothing burned—not the musicians, not their instruments, not even the sheet music. A police official and a civil engineer, both Englishmen, also crossed unharmed. "We felt we were in a furnace," they told the bishop, "but the fire did not burn us."

Intrigued by such anecdotal evidence, a number of scientists have sought to validate or refute the seemingly superhuman endurance displayed by fire walkers. In the spring of 1980, for example, a team of researchers from the University of Tübingen in West Germany joined the celebrants and sightseers who flocked to the annual festival of St. Constantine at Langadhas in northern Greece. A ritual fire walk was the high point of the festival, and the scientists, laden with equipment, were determined to put the participants under scrutiny.

First, they measured the fire pit at four yards in length, filled to a two-inch depth with coals whose surface temperature reached 932 degrees Fahrenheit. While celebrants in the background sacrificed young goats and danced to slowly beating drums, the scientists taped electrodes to the heads of three walkers to measure changes in brain-wave activity and attached thermocouples to their bare feet to take temperature readings.

Monitoring their instruments at the sidelines, the Germans observed the celebrants sauntering comfortably back and forth across the fire for a good quarter-hour without a sign of pain. One of the three subjects showed greatly increased theta-wave activity in the brain, a condition often associated with a sleeping or dreaming state; the others did not. The soles of their feet registered a temperature of only 356 degrees, about one-third that of the surface of the fire—but even so, their feet should have been broiled.

At the time, the experts from Tübingen were at a loss to explain what they had observed. But other experimenters have since developed theories of how fire walking might be managed. One, Dr. Jearl Walker, a professor of physics at Cleveland State University, invokes the "Leidenfrost effect," named for a German physician who first observed that a liquid exposed to intense heat will immediately form an insulating cushion of steam. Walker argues that perspiration on the feet, generated by excitement and the heat of the fire, protects them in the same way that a dab of saliva on the fingertips enables a person to touch a hot iron or snuff out a candle flame.

An alternate explanation has been offered by a pair of U.C.L.A. researchers, Bernard J. Leikind and William J. Mc-Carthy, who attended a Tony Robbins fire-walking seminar and came away unconvinced by Walker's theory. No armchair investigators, both men took the fiery plunge and walked away unharmed.

McCarthy, a psychologist, thought that the Robbins technique employed several pain-blocking techniques, from chanting to a particular style of breathing, that helped make the crossing endurable. And it is not by chance, he pointed out, that Robbins arranges his fire walks for the hours past midnight. "When we stay awake well past our normal bedtime," said McCarthy, "our normal physiological functions are nevertheless somewhat depressed—as if the body expected to be asleep even though it wasn't. The people who

walked on the coals at 1:00 a.m. were therefore much less likely to feel pain or heat than they would have been had they conducted the same walk at 1:00 p.m."

Leikind, a physicist, further concluded that the secret of fire walking lay in the distinction between temperature and heat, or inter-

Hiking her sari to protect it from the flames, a Hindu woman of Indian origin struts across a bed of glowing coals during an annual religious ceremony on the island nation of Mauritius.

A blazing towel attests to the heat as a Hindu mystic, Hatayogi Sandra Rao, walks on flaming embers without flinching during a 1966 demonstration in Bombay, India.

nal energy. "Different materials at the same temperature," he wrote, "contain different amounts of thermal or heat energy and have different abilities to carry the energy from one place to another." The embers used by fire walkers, he continued, are "light, fluffy carbon compounds. Although they may be at a fairly high temperature, they do not contain as much energy as we might expect."

The physicist drew a simple analogy. As a cake is baking, he pointed out, the metal cake pan and the air inside the oven are about the same temperature. Yet because the air has low heat energy and poor conductivity, the cook can safely put his hands inside the oven, while he would be ill-advised to touch the cake pan, which has much higher heat energy and conductivity. In the same way, Leikind contended, a bed of glowing coals may register a temperature of 1,000 degrees or more, but it will not feel nearly so hot to the feet as, say, a metal staircase heated to the same temperature—or, for that matter, a stretch of dry sand on an August afternoon at the beach.

Still, how is it that one person can negotiate a path of fire while another person, on the same trail, suffers severe burns? For this, too, Leikind suggests an answer: "Fire-walking is not a controlled scientific experiment. There are many variables from one person to the next and one moment to the next: how long we stay on the embers, how many steps we take, how tough the soles of our feet are, and whether we walk where the embers are deep or shallow. It certainly is possible to get injured, especially if we believe that it is our mind that protects us and if we do not take into account the normal physical behavior of heat."

Perhaps there is no way to fully measure the pain that is endured—and thus conquered—in fire walking. But there is no question that the body can be taught to absorb a degree of agony unimaginable to most people. This remarkable, if somewhat appalling, human capability is displayed the world over in countless ceremonies that center on the mortification and mutilation of the flesh.

One particularly awesome example takes place at the shrine of Kataragama in Sri Lanka, where the year-round

Crowds watch as Japanese priests negotiate a bed of coals in a yearly fire walk at a Buddhist shrine near Tokyo.

electrical energy of the nerves making up the brain. The electrical voltages generated by the nerves come in waves, the kind of wave at any given time being dependent on the mental state of the subject.

Four patterns of brain waves have been identified, each indicating a different level of mental activity. The pattern called alpha, characterized by crests of voltage peaking at a rate of about ten per second, usually occurs in an awake but relaxed person with eyes closed, so that visual impulses are blocked from the brain. The beta phase, in which the peaks are of lower voltage and come at a more rapid rate of thirteen to twenty-eight per second, is characteristic of an awake, attentive person engaged in some mental activity or operating under pressure. The slow theta waves, which alternate at about three to six per second, are usually apparent when the individual is asleep and dreaming but also occur during periods of creative thinking. The lowest-frequency waves, known as delta, are characteristic of deep sleep.

rituals of faith reach a climax in the dreadful ecstasies of August. As a temple bell tolls to welcome a dawn of almost unbearable heat, three silent men are scourged by lashes that lay open their flesh. A man stands motionless and uncomplaining as a long steel skewer is thrust into his cheek. Another methodically forces knives through the skin of his own legs and arms. In a separate group, a dozen or so individuals are inserting forty to fifty metal hooks, each attached to a sturdy cord, into the back of a devotee, after which they will hitch the man to a cart laden with offerings, to be dragged to the temple.

In the late 1970s, Dr. Wolfgang Larbig of the University of Tübingen attempted to analyze such gruesome self-mutilation by testing an accomplished Indian fakir, one of a class of mystics known for their ability to endure painful acts. For their experiment, Larbig and his associates used a number of test instruments, chief among them the electroencephalograph, or EEG, which measures the natural

In a preliminary demonstration of his skills, the fakir prepared himself for his ordeal by seemingly going into a trance. Then he nonchalantly thrust metal spikes into his stomach and neck and through his tongue. "From all overt behavioral indicators," the observers noted, "there was no evidence that he experienced any pain whatever." Nor was there any bleeding.

Larbig also called for volunteers to serve as control subjects. Fourteen responded and, like the fakir, were fitted with electrodes. All were told to expect pain and to prepare themselves mentally to bear it.

Larbig and his team administered some forty painful electric shocks to the fourteen volunteers and the fakir. When the test was over, the volunteers had obviously borne about as much pain as they could stand. The fakir, however, gazing heavenward, appeared impassive.

The brain waves recorded during the experiment showed an interesting disparity between those of the fakir and the sufferers. While the brain waves of the volunteers showed the expected response each time the painful shocks were administered, the fakir's brain waves showed a strong theta pattern—the slow frequency associated with drowsiness or dreaming—even when he felt the shock. It seemed as if he were deliberately inducing theta waves to deaden the pain. What is more, the conductivity of his skin during the experiment was altogether unlike that of the volunteers, presumably because the fakir had somehow willed in-

The Magic of Harry Houdini

The most renowned escape artist of all time was Harry Houdini, a Hungarian-born magician who dominated American show business during the first quarter of the twentieth century. Famous as "the man who could get out of anything," he would dazzle crowds of onlookers by plunging into a lake or an icy river with hands and feet manacled—only to wriggle free of his chains and pop to the surface unhurt. By his own count, he escaped this sort of drowning 2,000 times. Houdini never said he possessed supernatural powers. In fact, he took great pride in exposing the claims of fraudulent mediums and mystics. But he trained his body and mind with the rigor of an Indian yogi, cultivating the agility his escapes required and conditioning himself to withstand severe pain and to go long periods without breathing.

Born Ehrich Weiss in Budapest in 1874, Houdini was brought to the United States as an infant by his immigrant parents. He began his career as a small-time magician, playing dime museums and medicine shows. With characteristic bravado, he borrowed his stage name from Jean Eugène Robert Houdin, the most famous French magician of the 1800s. But he soon largely abandoned conjuring, focusing his act instead on his amazing ability to shed manacles and chains, and it was as an escape artist that he became a headliner in the top vaudeville theaters of America as well as a wildly popular attraction in the music halls of Europe. He publicized his performances not only by plunging into rivers while manacled, but also by escaping from straitjackets, packing boxes, locked trunks, and even from death-row cells in federal and state prisons.

One of Houdini's most celebrated feats was not an escape but rather a demonstration of controlled breathing. In 1926, he read about an Egyptian fakir who claimed supernatural powers and had survived being underwater in a sealed coffin for an hour. The fakir, Rahman Bey,

Famous for his hypnotic stare, Houdini's large head and strong features made him look like a Roman consul—and helped him become a star of silent films.

said that the feat could be achieved only by attaining a state of suspended animation in which respiration ceased. Houdini, always an enemy of those he considered frauds, decided to prove Bey wrong.

Using a specially made, casket-size tin box, Houdini trained even more energetically than usual for three weeks. Never one to take unnecessary risks, he had the box equipped with a phone so that he could keep an open line to his longtime assistant, Jimmy Collins, in case of an emergency. On August 5 he lay down in the box, the lid was tightly screwed on and soldered, and he was lowered into the swimming pool of New York's Shelton Hotel *(opposite)*.

After fifty minutes he informed Collins that he was breathing heavily and was "not sure of staying an hour." But stay he did—past the hour that Rahman Bey had remained submerged, past an hour and a quarter. Despite a leak that was letting in water, Houdini remained calm, breathing at a normal rate of seventeen times a minute. Finally after an hour and a half he told Collins to raise the box, which was swiftly cut open by workmen. Houdini emerged wet and exhausted, but still displayed his showman's flair by taking several deep breaths, flexing his muscles, and announcing that he felt fine.

Some of Rahman Bey's followers accused Houdini of concealing oxygen-liberating chemicals in the box or perpetrating some other trickery. Houdini replied that no tricks were needed—aside from the ability to banish fear, remain calm, and conserve oxygen through breath control. Examination of the box showed that Houdini had employed no artificial aids.

Houdini died less than three months afterward, a victim of his fame and his own iron will. A young man who had heard of Houdini's ability to withstand any blow by hardening his stomach muscles punched him in the abdomen—when he was not ready. The blows caused severe internal damage, but Houdini fiercely ignored the pain for days while his condition worsened. When he finally collapsed and was taken to a hospital, it was too late. He succumbed to peritonitis on October 31, 1926, at the age of fifty-two.

Showing little strain after ninety minutes underwater in a sealed box, Harry Houdini emerges from the coffin hoisted from the Shelton Hotel swimming pool in New York (below). During his ordeal, teams of assistants had to hold the buoyant container under the surface to keep it fully submerged (inset, left).

to existence some sort of a barrier against the pain.

The experimenters concluded that the fakir, by apparently simple techniques of meditation, was able to produce measurable changes in body and brain to inhibit the sensation of pain. What they could not explain was why no blood had been drawn by the deep perforations from the metal spikes, or why only faint marks were left instead of wounds.

Something similar, and yet in one respect surprisingly different, had occurred a few years earlier in the laboratory of American researchers Elmer and Alyce Green. Their subject was Jack Schwarz, a naturalized American born in the same region of the Netherlands as Peter Hurkos, who gained worldwide fame for his alleged psychic abilities. Completely without training in the field of meditation, Schwarz claimed to have discovered in himself an unexpected wealth of extraordinary talents. He could stab himself without bleeding, he said; he could prevent or stop his sensations of pain; he could alleviate pain in others by placing his hands on them; he could hypnotize people; and he could read minds.

In the laboratory, Schwarz was hooked up to record several physiological variables—among them heart rate, breathing rate, and skin temperature—that indicate stress reactions. He then proceeded to give a vivid demonstration of his ability to control bleeding. Schwarz had brought with him a pair of six-inch sailmaker's needles; now he explained that he planned to push them through his biceps and yank them out, bloodlessly. Once he had thrust one of the needles into his arm, however, Elmer Green threw him a curve. "I decided that it would be useful for the record if it were demonstrated that Jack could bleed in a normal way," he wrote later, "or merely had a peculiar skin." So, just as Schwarz was about to pull the needle from his arm, Green interrupted him and said, "Jack, tell me, is it going to bleed now?" Schwarz, caught off guard, pulled the needle out, leaving a wound that gushed blood for about ten seconds while Green tried to swab it with tissues.

"Then," according to Green, "I heard Jack say very softly, 'Now it stops.' Much to my surprise, the hole in the skin that I was dabbing closed up as if drawn by purse strings. It took about one second to close, and not another drop of blood appeared."

When the experiment continued, Schwarz was asked to pierce himself again but not to bleed at all. He pushed one of the huge needles through another arm muscle, let it remain there for about thirty seconds, then pulled it out. No blood appeared, even though Green vigorously squeezed the place where the needle had been.

Two things in this experiment were particularly interesting to the investigators. One was Schwarz's observation that in such a demonstration he gave no more thought to his arm than if it were the arm of a stuffed chair. Apparently, he did so without knowing that such mental detachment is a well-known method of yogic control and a frequent accompaniment to the production of alpha waves.

The other significant point was his brain-wave pattern. While waiting for the experiment to begin, Schwarz emitted beta waves almost constantly. "We considered this quite normal under the circumstances," reported the Greens. "We expected him to be activated. When he put the tip of the needle to his biceps, however, his brain-wave record began to show alpha. This was exactly the opposite from what the average person could be expected to do. A person sitting in a quiet room with nothing to do will usually begin to produce alpha, but if he were asked to push a needle through his arm he would be expected to abruptly block alpha and produce beta." What Schwarz appeared to be doing was turning his attention away from the sensation of pain. He simply removed himself from it.

Just as the human mind can steel itself to overcome its own fears or the weaknesses of the body, so can it seemingly bring about injury where no physical cause is evident. A singularly dramatic manifestation of this capability—the spontaneous appearance on the body of stigmata, the bleeding wounds of Christ—has been occurring at odd times and places since it was first experienced by St. Francis of Assisi more than 700 years ago.

A case often cited is that of Louise Lateau, a Belgian peasant of the nineteenth century who was accustomed to seeing visions of various saints—some of them quite obscure—and falling into ecstatic trances or fits of what might today be termed hysteria. One Friday in 1868, the stigmata were visited upon Louise for the first time, bloodying her hands and feet and the area beneath her left breast. This phenomenon accorded in nearly every respect with the traditional Christian belief that the wounds of Christ at the Crucifixion appeared on the hands, the feet, the forehead, and the left side of the body.

Thereafter, the events recurred on an eerily reliable weekly cycle. On Tuesdays Louise would begin to feel burning sensations in the areas where the stigmata were to appear. On Thursday evenings the pain would begin. On Friday mornings blisters emerged and enlarged until they burst and bled. At this, Louise would take a communion wafer, pray, fall into a trance, and finally lie facedown on the floor until the spell seemed to subside. Then she would rise to her feet. By the next day the bloody blisters would be gone, leaving only patches of pale pink that disappeared by the following Tuesday, when the burning began again.

Even apart from this regularly scheduled hemorrhaging, Louise Lateau was an unusual young woman, fervent in her piety and given to long, solitary sessions of meditation and prayer. She was also, like most of those visited with stigmata, a white, adult Roman Catholic. Cloretta Robertson, by contrast, was black and Baptist. A few weeks before Easter in 1972, the ten-year-old Oakland, California, schoolgirl was sitting in a classroom when she noticed that the palm of her left hand was bleeding. She felt no pain, and there were no apparent marks on her hand. When the mysterious bleeding continued to occur sporadically over the following three days, the girl was taken to a pediatrician, Loretta F. Early, who found that the skin on Cloretta's palm was normal and showed no injuries. Nevertheless, the physician bound the young patient's left hand securely with a surgical dressing before sending her back to school. Three hours later, while Cloretta was sitting in her classroom, blood appeared on the palm of her right hand.

In the days that followed, the inexplicable bleeding continued—from the girl's feet, chest, and forehead as well as from her hands. Still, Dr. Early could find no signs of injury on her patient's skin. Psychiatrist Joseph E. Lifschutz was called in, and although he did not subject Cloretta to extensive testing, he detected no obvious indications that the girl suffered from severe personality disorders. She was, however, extremely religious, although she claimed never to have heard of such a thing as stigmata until after her own bleeding had occurred.

On Good Friday, Cloretta Robertson's bleeding stopped, and it did not recur during the following Easter season. Meanwhile, Early and Lifschutz continued to study the case and the stigmata phenomenon in general. Reporting on their findings in a psychiatric journal, they observed that it was virtually impossible that Cloretta had somehow wounded herself—a suspicion that arises, naturally enough, in any such instance. On the other hand, they noted, "one can no longer dispute the power of mental and emotional forces to control such physical phenomena." There could be no doubt, they said, that "profound, intense religious and emotional forces, conscious and unconscious, could cause stigmatic bleeding."

At least as baffling are cases of stigmata that seem to have no religious motivation. For example, a nineteenth-century Swedish physician named Magnus Huss was examining a twenty-three-year-old Swedish woman—identified in his report only as Maria K.—who had been severely beaten. Long after Maria's wounds had healed, blood continued to appear from her ears, eyes, and other places on the head, although there were no marks on the skin except for traces of inflammation. In time Dr. Huss found that Maria could stimulate bleeding whenever she wished, simply by getting into an argument with someone and working herself up to an emotional pitch.

Similarly, in 1969 Dr. Oscar Ratnoff, professor of medicine at Case Western Reserve University in Cleveland, was

In this painting by the fourteenth-century Italian artist Giotto, St. Francis of Assisi receives the stigmata directly from Christ. The first recorded sufferer from such wounds, St. Francis is said to have begun bleeding from his hands and feet while praying outside a cave in the year 1224.

working with an emotionally distressed patient when he observed the appearance on the woman's thigh of a globule of blood the size of a silver dollar. There was no evident cause, and when the blood was wiped away no wound was disclosed. The only clue was her mental anguish. Fascinated, Ratnoff eventually found and investigated more than sixty patients who periodically developed welts, bruises, and bleeding for no discernible reason. Although there may be other explanations—some researchers have suggested sensitivity to an element in one's own blood—Ratnoff became convinced that these effects were triggered by the emotions of the patients. Most, he found, were battered or otherwise abused women, many of them emotionally disturbed and suffering, as Ratnoff put it, from "more than their share of the griefs of the living." Somehow, he concluded, they had managed to reproduce their mental scars on the surface of their bodies.

To be sure, those people are rare who, driven by religious passion or some secret torment, can thus mysteriously display their suffering for all to see. Rarer still, perhaps, are their opposites—those who become so adroit at summoning and deploying their mental energy that they can seemingly flout physical laws as they wish. And there may well be no better illustration of such singular talents than Daniel Dunglas Home, the preeminent medium of the nineteenth century.

Home's abilities were indeed prodigious. He dazzled Europe, including the royal courts of Napoleon III and Czar Alexander II, with his occult skills—daring, for example, to lead séances in daylight rather than in the darkness favored by other mediums of the day. In small, informal demonstrations for friends, he would plunge his hands and even his face into a hearth fire, "moving it about as though bathing it in water," wrote one nonplussed observer. Home's little performances were the outlandish stuff of fairy tales. There were reputable people who swore that he had stretched himself, before their eyes, so as to add six inches to his height, or that he had set an accordion to swinging about

Father Pio Forgione of Foggia, Italy, celebrates Mass for a number of his followers, who revered him as a stigmatic. From the time the stigmata appeared in 1915 until his death in 1968, Forgione bled almost daily from the traditional sites of Christ's wounds.

a room, playing a sprightly tune with no one at the keys.

But the feat that gained for Home the greatest renown—and, among the legion of doubters, the greatest infamy—occurred on December 13, 1868, at Home's apartment at Ashley House in the Westminster borough of London. In attendance were three distinguished young observers—Viscount Adare, then twenty-seven years old, who would become the fourth earl of Dunraven and a correspondent for the London *Daily Telegraph;* James Ludovic Lindsay, twenty-one, a future president of the Royal Astronomical Society and trustee of the British Museum; and Captain Charles Bradstreet Wynne, thirty-three, Adare's cousin and a military officer stationed at the Tower of London. Both Adare and Lindsay gave extensive written accounts of what they believed Home did that night. "When one considers the standing of the three eyewitnesses who have testified to this," said Sir Arthur Conan Doyle, the British author and spiritualist, "one may well ask whether in ancient or modern times any preternatural event has been more clearly proved." Perhaps so, but it still requires a considerable leap of the imagination to accept Home's claimed accomplishment: that in the early evening of that Sunday, he levitated himself from a standing position, floated out of the room and through a window, and returned through a window in the first room. "We heard Home go into the next room, heard the window thrown up, and presently Home appeared standing upright outside our window," Lindsay recalled. "He remained in this position for a few seconds, then raised the window and glided into the room feet foremost and sat down."

Then and now, many experts in psychic matters who generally credit Home's achievements look askance at the Ashley House levitation. They point out that Home's exit through the window was unwitnessed. In fact, the medium had specifically asked the three observers not to leave their chairs in the other room. Close examination of photographs of the building (which has long since been razed) shows balconies outside each window, a little more than four feet apart—a distance that could easily be leaped by a man with no fear of heights, such as Home was. He could have climbed out one of the third-floor windows and jumped from balcony to balcony.

This scenario leaves unanswered the question of how Home could have returned to his three friends by drifting unsupported through the open window into their room as they looked on. Some critics reply that in the near-total darkness of the room, Home could have simply climbed through the window without giving himself away. Others, pointing to multiple contradictions in the eyewitness accounts, contend that Lindsay and Adare in particular, through constant exposure to the charismatic medium, had become susceptible to whatever he told them. "I think the only valid explanation," wrote the British author Trevor Hall, who in the 1980s conducted a lengthy inquiry into the incident, "is that the observers must have been in a mildly abnormal state throughout the sitting and generally during their association with Home, who was one of those rare in-

An old illustration shows St. Joseph of Copertino levitating during a religious rapture. The monk's ability to fly was reportedly verified by many seventeenth-century notables.

dividuals who possess the power of imposing suggestion upon others to a marked degree." Hall came to the conclusion that "the Ashley House levitation was an ingenious fraud purposefully perpetrated by Home for his own advantage."

Bogus or not, the 1868 levitation had followed many others, more modest in scale, that Home had executed before hundreds of people. He recounted these brief flights in his 1863 autobiography, *Incidents in My Life*. "During these elevations or levitations," he explained, "I usually experience in my body no particular sensation other than what I could only describe as an electrical fullness about the feet. I feel no hands supporting me, and since the first time have never felt fear. . . . My arms frequently become rigid, and are drawn above my head, as if I were grasping the unseen power which slowly raised me from the floor."

That unseen power has apparently been felt by mystics of every stripe throughout history, from the ecstatic transports of the saints to the meditative levitations of the yogis of India and their Western disciples. St. Joseph of Copertino was a celebrated Italian levitator of the seventeenth century who, according to legend, was able to rise into the air whenever he was emotionally excited. He had no control over his flights and sometimes found himself in precarious positions. Once, at a Sunday Mass, he reportedly soared into the air and floated to the altar. On a later occasion, while St. Joseph walked with a Benedictine monk in the monastery garden, he suddenly rose high into an olive tree. There he remained, unable to descend, while the monk went in search of a ladder.

Two saintly women also figure in the annals of levitation. One, St. Teresa of Avila, who lived in the sixteenth century, said of her experience: "It seemed to me, when I tried to make some resistance, as if a great force beneath my feet lifted me up. I confess that it threw me into great fear, very great indeed at first; for in seeing one's body thus lifted up from the earth, though the spirit draws it upwards after itself (and that with great sweetness, if unresisted) the senses are not lost; at least I was so much myself as able to see that I was being lifted up."

A note of practicality was introduced into such sublime experiences about 200 years later by a visionary nun named Anne Catherine Emmerich, who described her manner of housekeeping: "I was often lifted up suddenly into the air, and I climbed up and stood on the higher parts of the church, such as windows, sculptured ornaments, jutting stones. I would clean and arrange everything in places where it was humanly impossible. I felt myself lifted and supported in the air, and I was not afraid in the least, for I had been accustomed from a child to being assisted by my guardian angel."

If levitation came naturally, even unbidden, to Sister Anne Catherine, St. Teresa, and St. Joseph, such an experience is the exception. In the centuries-old yogic tradition of India, there are eight great *siddhis,* or accomplishments, of which levitation is only one. Long instruction and practice in techniques of breathing, relaxation, and posture are needed before one can hope to levitate.

The results of all this discipline can be striking. In the nineteenth century, for example, European travelers to India came home bursting with tales like those related in Olivier Leroy's 1928 book, *Levitation.* As he told it, a Frenchman living in Pondicherry in 1866 reported seeing a fakir named

Covindassamy suspended two feet above the earth. Another time the same fakir visited the Frenchman for lunch and upon leaving was lifted about one foot from the ground, where he stayed, motionless, for about five minutes.

India has remained the world center of supposed levitation, although some practitioners of the art have sought to export their knowledge to the West. Maharishi Mahesh Yogi, perhaps the modern world's most celebrated guru, or spiritual guide, began teaching courses in levitation at his very expensive Swiss academy in 1976, as an extension of his teachings in Transcendental Meditation—familiarly

Daniel Dunglas Home, the famous Scots-born medium of the nineteenth century, floats to the ceiling during one of the many levitations he is said to have performed before groups of witnesses.

known as TM. On May 16, 1977, the London *Evening News* reported that twelve students had graduated from the maharishi's first six-month course. One newly minted adept, Albertine Haupt, was quoted as saying: "I suddenly found myself six feet above the floor and thought, 'Heavens, I've done it!' " Apparently, the descent was more difficult than the flight; she and the other students reportedly landed unceremoniously and, despite plentiful foam-rubber padding, sustained a number of minor bruises.

Albertine Haupt did not reveal her technique. But another TM graduate explained, a bit hazily: "People would rock gently, then more and more, and then start lifting off into the air. . . . Then you learn to control it better, and it becomes totally exhilarating." For such students, it seemed no great trial to achieve a state of semiweightlessness through meditation and thus be capable of levitation.

One devotee of yoga and meditation, Steve Richards, described the method more fully in a book titled *Levitation,* like Olivier Leroy's. Noting that breath control for occult purposes underlies a science known as *pranayama,* Richards went on to explain that "levitation comes from pranayama, and pranayama comes from control of an energy in the air called prana . . . energy in its purest form." The power of mind over matter is possible, he declared, "because prana not only controls mind; prana *is* mind."

To achieve levitation, Richards wrote, students must sit in the cross-legged position known as full lotus. They must learn to breathe properly, in the manner described by yogis as diaphragmatic breathing—which involves building up the ability to hold one's breath. Systematic deep relaxation must be learned and practiced and ultimately combined with the pranayama cycle of inhalation, breath retention, and exhalation. As one traditional yogic text, the Siva Samhita, describes the process, "In the first stage of pranayama the body of the yogi begins to perspire. In the second stage, there takes place the trembling of the body; in the third, the jumping about like a frog; and when the practice becomes greater, the adept walks in the air."

Transcendental Meditation, as taught by the maharishi, may or may not give physical elevation to its practitioners—leaders of the discipline have been chary of subjecting their methods to scientific observation, and some critics who have seen photographs of alleged levitations maintain that the feats appear to be nothing more than a kind of cross-legged hopping into the air. But TM does appear capable of producing a pronounced feeling of mental exhilaration. According to the maharishi, it is a way for the individual to tap vast inner resources, a reservoir of "unlimited energy, intelligence, power, peace and bliss." When a person begins to use this potential, the maharishi says, "all aspects of his life flourish, in the same way that the branches, fruits and leaves of a tree flourish when the roots maintain contact with the field of nourishment in the soil."

As simple as it may appear to the uninitiated, practitioners of TM maintain that the techniques of relaxation and levitation can be learned only from an instructor trained by the maharishi himself. After a series of introductory lectures, the students undergo a weeks-long course detailing the goals and principles of meditation, after which they are able to meditate alone. Each time they practice TM, students must mentally repeat a specific sound or word, known as a mantra, chosen by the instructor and supposedly tailored to the individual's special qualities.

As a method of relaxation, this silent repetition of a word—whether or not it is called a mantra—has been widely employed outside of the formal realms of Transcendental Meditation. The nineteenth-century English poet Alfred, Lord Tennyson, for example, was a regular user of the technique. In a letter to a friend, he wrote: "A kind of waking trance—this for lack of a better word—I have frequently had, quite up from boyhood, when I have been all alone. This has come upon me through repeating my own name to myself silently, till all at once . . . individuality itself seemed to dissolve and fade away into boundless being, and this not a confused state but the clearest, the surest of the surest, utterly beyond words."

Apparently, states of mental bliss are not the only ef-

His hand resting lightly atop a cloth-covered stick, Indian yogi Subbayah Pullavar appears to float above the ground in this 1936 photograph taken by a British traveler. Pullavar's assistants hid him from view with a tent during the alleged levitation and the descent.

fects that can be achieved in such ways. During the early 1970s, Dr. Herbert Benson, a cardiologist at the Harvard University Medical School, was researching the relationship between stress and hypertension. He speculated that if stress could produce bodily changes such as faster breathing and increases in blood pressure and pulse rate, then some other factor might be able to do the opposite. He studied several practitioners of TM and determined that by chanting a word or sound—for his experiments, he chose "om," a popular, all-purpose mantra—under quiet, comfortable conditions, some subjects in a meditative state could actually lower their blood pressure, breathing, and pulse rates at will.

Practitioners of Transcendental Meditation, among them business executives, artists, and college students, have reported experiencing less tension, less worry, and generally better health. "For the first time since I can re-member," said one, "I can relax, really relax, without drugs or drink." Some stated that they had found relief from such ailments as eyestrain, migraines, and asthma. Others, turning to a somewhat similar technique, have reported even more dramatic results.

While in Texas on a convention trip with her husband in the 1970s, Mrs. Donald Wildowsky dived into a swimming pool and ruptured an eardrum. "We were miles from any town," she said after returning to her home back east, "and I didn't want to make [Donald] leave in the middle of the convention. So I went to an alpha state, put my hand over my ear, concentrated on the pain area and said, 'Gone, gone, gone!' The bleeding stopped immediately and the pain left."

Wildowsky was practicing the Silva Mind Control Method, which teaches that the brain-wave pattern known as alpha reflects a state of "inner consciousness." Many

things can allegedly be achieved in this state, including a measure of self-healing.

In another such reported instance, a Detroit nun, Sister Barbara Burns, was suffering from nearsighted astigmatism and had worn increasingly stronger eyeglasses over the course of twenty-seven years. As the lenses became more powerful her ability to see at a distance decreased and she started wearing bifocals. Then, in July 1974, she decided to try Silva Mind Control. After achieving a state of deep meditation, she told herself, "Every time I blink my eyes, they will focus accurately, like the lens of a camera." She repeated this to herself during each meditation. In two weeks, she said, she gave up using her glasses for everything but reading. When her optometrist, himself a practitioner of the Silva system, informed her that her cornea was slightly misshapen, Sister Barbara simply changed her meditation to include the desired cornea correction. When she returned to the optometrist a year later, she said, she was found not to need glasses at all.

The Silva Mind Control Method is one of the most popular of the many such systems that emerged in the 1960s and 1970s. Like Transcendental Meditation and other techniques that are said to improve mental and physical health, it involves a form of relaxation and meditation. But while TM considers tranquillity and inner peace its goals, Silva sees those qualities as ways to reach specific goals in the external world. A person properly trained in Silva principles is promised that he or she will be able to perceive dangers ahead, win lotteries, find misplaced items, cure addictions, and achieve countless other desirable aims.

José Silva, who formulated the system that bears his name, was born in Laredo, Texas, in 1914 and rose from poverty to establish a thriving electronics business. At the same time, he was indulging a more compelling interest: the study of hypnosis to improve learning ability. Could the IQ, Silva wondered, be improved through mental training? When his children began bringing home a few too many failing grades on their report cards, he tried to determine whether hypnosis could calm their minds and increase their ability to absorb information. His conclusion seems paradoxical: When the brain is less active, according to Silva, it is actually more energetic; it admits and retains more information in a placid state. What the less active mind does not do, however, is keep alert in such areas as insight, understanding, and independent thought.

Psychologists, neurologists, and others might raise their eyebrows at such notions, but Silva was convinced. He abandoned hypnosis and, melding precepts of Eastern and Western learning, developed a set of mental training exercises intended to relax the mind while still leaving it alert. By dint of what he called "relaxed concentration" and "mental visualization," he found, people can bring themselves to just the proper level of awareness.

Silva's rigorous, four- or five-day course offers several techniques for tapping into that level. And then, he advises, "from the very first moment you reach your meditative level, practice visualization. This is central to Mind Control." According to Silva, those seeking to accomplish visualization should start off by mentally projecting a simple image—an orange or an apple will do—on an imaginary screen about six feet in front of them. They should then concentrate on making the picture more and more real, more and more vivid. With practice, more complex images—even events—can be projected.

The next and most crucial step is to transform the imaginary situation into a real one. To achieve this, Silva says, a person must desire that the event take place, must believe that the event can take place, and must expect that the event will take place. A salesman, for example, might prepare for a crucial presentation by imagining himself making a persuasive sales pitch that clinches the deal; a cabdriver experiencing a slow day with few fares would think of someone with suitcases who wants to be taken to a distant airport.

Silva cheerfully concedes that his system is not totally original, and he acknowledges his debt of gratitude to Dr. Émile Coué, a French chemist turned psychotherapist who

The Bow of Self-Mastery

Archery is still widely practiced in Japan, but the main object is not to develop skill in hitting the target. Rather, the primary purpose of what is called *kyudo,* or "the way of the bow," is to achieve self-mastery through a perfect integration of mind and body, arrow and bow. The adept, such as the archer seen at right, is supposed to acquire not only graceful shooting form, but also the sort of egoless serenity that is the goal of the ancient Buddhist-derived philosophy of Zen. In *kyudo,* its practitioners say, "the target is one's mind. The archer confronts his inner self."

Handling a bow was originally a purely military skill; but as early as the eighth century, Japanese nobility recognized that archery was a way of teaching self-discipline. When Buddhism reached Japan about the twelfth century, archery was transformed into *kyudo,* seen as a path to spiritual knowledge. And long after firearms had supplanted the bow, it was still practiced by Zen monks and members of the ruling class as a mental, physical, and spiritual exercise. Even today as many as 70,000 archers are registered in Japan, most studying under *kyudo* masters.

Breath control is a prerequisite for good shooting. So is the proper handling of the huge, asymmetrical bow, which may be up to seven and a half feet long. Most important, the masters say, is to achieve a state of mind that is at once relaxed and intensely aware. The release of the arrow ideally comes at a time of such mental peace—of unconscious readiness—that the archer is not totally aware he is letting go. "The shot will only go smoothly," a Zen adage says, "when it takes the archer himself by surprise." Such a shot, *kyudo* adepts aver, will more often than not strike the bull's-eye, although such success is relatively unimportant. The bow, as another adage has it, "is simply a tool to cleanse one's mind."

held forth at a free clinic in Nancy from 1910 until his death in 1926. By all reports, Coué successfully treated thousands of patients suffering from a range of afflictions, from rheumatism and asthma to paralysis and tumors.

Coué's medicine was a form of self-hypnosis, and he is remembered today for the singsong formula he urged his patients to repeat and take to heart: "Day by day, in every way, I am getting better and better." According to Silva, Coué never took credit for curing anyone; he taught his patients to cure themselves. "It is a simple method," Silva has written. "Everyone can learn it. The heart of it is in Mind Control. There are two basic principles: (1) We can think of only one thing at a time, and (2) When we concentrate on a thought, the thought becomes true because our bodies transform it into action."

Naturally, such systems as TM and Silva Mind Control are not without their critics, many of whom are quick to point out the lack of medical or scientific credentials among so many of those who have developed the techniques. Indeed, José Silva, for one, boasts that he had no formal education at all save for a correspondence course in radio repair. Beyond that, the critics say, there is scant clinical evidence that the production of certain types of brain waves is directly responsible for any particularly beneficial state of consciousness. In most cases, they contend, the al-

leged therapeutic benefits of Transcendental Meditation and similar mental techniques can be achieved equally well if a person simply sits with closed eyes and confidently expects the desired result.

Doubters have raised similar objections to some of the claims made for hypnosis, the sleeplike state that renders subjects susceptible to suggestions of various kinds. Indeed, for many, hypnotism has acquired an air of quackery, thanks chiefly to the numerous stage magicians who, over the years, have supposedly "mesmerized" audience members and persuaded them to do such bizarre things as cluck like chickens or bark like dogs. This antic behavior aside, however, few people will do anything while under hypnosis that goes against their basic moral principles. Nor is a specially trained operator always required to put someone into a hypnotic state. Most people, in fact, can hypnotize themselves. As the parapsychologist and accomplished hypnotist Leslie M. LeCron put it, "Essentially all hypnosis is self-hypnosis. The operator is merely a guide and the subject produces a result."

According to LeCron, "The main purpose of self-

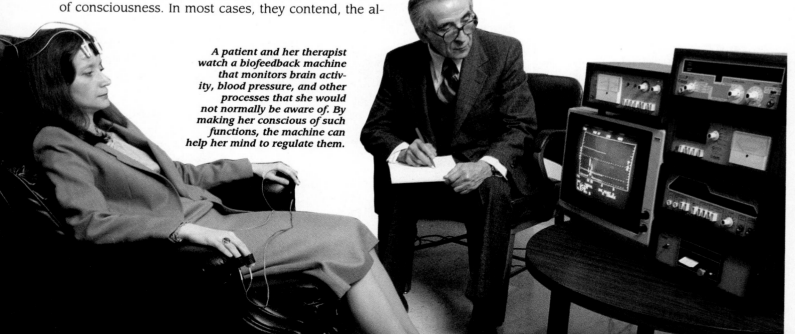

A patient and her therapist watch a biofeedback machine that monitors brain activity, blood pressure, and other processes that she would not normally be aware of. By making her conscious of such functions, the machine can help her mind to regulate them.

hypnosis is to influence the inner mind through suggestion, which will greatly shorten the time in reaching your goals in any program of self-therapy." Once a suggestion is planted, advocates of this practice say, self-hypnosis can work to stave off fatigue, replenish vigor and vitality, and block the pain of migraine headaches, arthritis, and many another ailment. Obstetricians who practice hypnosis can teach it to their patients, who in turn can induce calm when the time comes for delivery. Indeed, some studies show that self-hypnosis can trigger surprising physiological changes: lowering or raising body temperature, increasing the rate of healing, slowing or speeding the heartbeat, repairing the errant action of glands and organs. By far the most common use of self-hypnosis, however, is to relieve insomnia and alleviate minor pain.

While it is popularly thought of as a sleeping or unconscious state, there is no loss of consciousness in hypnosis. Rather, subjects are in a mildly altered state of consciousness—comparable, perhaps, to daydreaming. Although they are able to block out extraneous matters and concentrate on specific goals, they are completely aware of what they are saying and doing.

The usual way to learn the technique is to be hypnotized first by a therapist and then given posthypnotic suggestions for inducing the hypnotic state in oneself. LeCron, however, suggested an alternative method. "For practice in self-induction," he wrote, "it is best at first to use some object for eye fixation. When you have become proficient this will not be necessary. Almost anything will do—a picture on the wall, a spot on the ceiling, anything you can look at without discomfort."

LeCron especially recommended the flickering flame of a candle for its hypnotic effect and advised would-be self-hypnotists to sit in a comfortable position while they watched the flame. "Give yourself suggestions by thinking them," he wrote. "One suggestion might be, 'As I watch this candle my eyelids will become heavier and heavier. Soon they will be so heavy that they will close. Soon I will be in hypnosis.'" LeCron continued, "As your eyes close, you should have a key word or phrase ready to serve as a signal to your subconscious to bring you into hypnosis. A good one is 'relax now.' The 'now' in this phrase is important because it means immediately, not sometime later."

Subjects are then advised to relax their muscles, let their breathing become ever slower, and think, "Now I am going deeper and deeper." As they enter the stage of deep relaxation they should suggest to themselves that they will return to wakefulness spontaneously after a certain period of time. Then, they should mentally step off into the depths of whatever they feel is a relaxing, pleasant place.

Self-hypnosis, according to LeCron, is the best cure available for insomnia. He advised insomniacs to put themselves into hypnosis as they go to bed and then suggest to themselves that within a few minutes they will drift enjoyably into natural slumber for the rest of the night.

More unusual and impressive than this soporific application are the therapeutic uses of hypnosis in cases of extreme illness. Dr. Milton H. Erickson, a physician who died in 1980, was known for his uncommon therapies and was often called upon to offer relief in cases of excruciating terminal illness. In one instance, a woman dying of uterine cancer was being kept in a near stupor by constant doses of pain-killing drugs. This treatment greatly distressed the patient and her family; with her death imminent, they wanted to spend as much time as possible communicating with each other. The woman's doctor suggested hypnosis and asked Erickson to step in.

Asking that no narcotics be administered on the chosen day of treatment, Erickson worked with the patient for four hours at a stretch, as he reported afterward, "systematically teaching her, despite her attacks of pain, to go into a trance, to develop a numbness of her body, to absorb herself in a state of profound fatigue so that she could have physiological sleep despite the pain."

Erickson continued, "I also trained her to respond hypnotically to her husband, her oldest daughter and her family physician so that hypnosis could be reinforced in the

Daredevil motorcyclist Evel Knievel approaches his landing ramp
after soaring over a lineup of seventeen parked cars in a 1971 stunt. Knievel, who retired in 1974,
always envisioned a perfect jump before roaring up the takeoff ramp.

event of any new development when I was not there. Only this one long hypnotic session was required. She could discontinue her medication except for one heavy hypodermic administered late on a Thursday evening, which gave her additional relief and allowed her to be in full contact with her family in a rested state on the weekends. She also shared in the family evening activities during the week.

"Six weeks after her first trance, while talking to her daughter, she suddenly lapsed into a coma. She died two days later without recovering consciousness."

Even though it is being put to new and significant uses, hypnotism itself remains virtually the same practice it was centuries ago *(pages 90-101).* But there is still another avenue to the mental and physical fulfillment promised by hypnosis, one that could only have come into being in the technological age.

Since the 1960s, a number of researchers have been using a system called biofeedback to train people to control physiological functions long assumed to be involuntary—except in the cases of Muslim or Hindu fakirs and a few mystifying individuals like Jack Schwarz, who could open a wound without bleeding. At the heart of this technique is an array of devices designed to detect and monitor various physical states and activity, including temperature, blood pressure, heartbeat, and muscular contraction. Together, the equipment provides a huge volume of fairly simple information about the functioning of complicated body systems.

Barbara Brown, a pioneer in biofeedback applications, has pointed out that physicians usually interpret such data in order to gauge wellness or illness. "If, however," she says, "*you* are permitted to read that same information about yourself, you interpret the information in a frame of reference about how you feel inside. That is biofeedback: you are being fed back biological information about your biological self."

The biofeedback subject, sitting or lying in a comfortable position, is linked by delicate sensory equipment to a screen that displays a continuous commentary on a partic-

ular inner function, such as blood pressure or muscle contraction. The trainee is instructed to tell his body what to do—decrease blood pressure, for example—and then relax. A light or a sound from the monitor indicates the measure of success. In time, the subject learns to associate the way he feels with the response he is getting.

As Brown describes the process, a subject can "identify the feelings he has when the body is signaling the monitor device to say 'blood pressure up,' or 'blood pressure down,' or 'heart rate up,' or 'temperature down,' or 'more alpha.' It is very simple as a part-psychologic, part-medical compass on the road to satisfyingly better physical and mental health."

Biofeedback training sessions take place over several weeks, even months. Many patients also practice at home, using a portable biofeedback device. Eventually, when the trainee has mastered the process, the apparatus can be dispensed with altogether. In one notable case in 1975, a woman came to the world-renowned Menninger Clinic in Topeka, Kansas, to consult Elmer Green, a biofeedback specialist who headed the psychophysiology laboratory there. She was suffering from tachycardia, or rapid heartbeat, and great anxiety—not only about the possibility of death, but also about the stresses of daily life. In any given six weeks, she would have to be rushed to a hospital emergency room two or three times.

Within several weeks, Green related later, his new patient had learned relaxation and breathing techniques that permitted her to find deep calm whenever her heart reacted abnormally to any form of stress. "Her reports indicated that she was able to use her training in many ways," Green said. "A brief use of the breathing and relaxation techniques helped her control her pulse rate and handle pressures of hurrying and of parties and other social engagements. By nature an emotional person, she told of handling various reactions in calmer ways, having 'a better temper.'

"She reported waking up one morning with a very severe headache. She sat up to reach for some medication on her nightstand, then thought, 'No, I'll use my exercises.' In

20 minutes her headache was gone; she slept soundly and awakened refreshed."

A month later the woman saw her cardiologist, who was pleased to find that the condition of her heart had improved and even more pleased to learn that she had not visited the emergency room since starting biofeedback training. "She told him that she could intentionally slow her heart," Green reported, "but when he said 'All right, show me,' and placed his fingers on her pulse, she thought, 'What have I done? Now I am frightened, how can I slow my heart?' She closed her eyes and thought, 'Body, don't go back on me now,' took several deep, even breaths, and then began repeating silently, 'My heartbeat is slow and calm, my heartbeat is slow and calm.' Soon he stopped her, saying, 'Yes, you are slowing your heart rate.' In spite of the challenging situation, she had succeeded."

By the end of her training she had lowered her heart rate still further and had reduced her medication considerably. There were no more late-night trips to the hospital. In addition, she had gained an impressive degree of social poise; was no longer afraid of flying; was no longer even afraid of death.

"I explained again," said Green, "what I had often explained before: that whatever had been accomplished in her had been accomplished by *her*, that biofeedback instruments are just sophisticated mirrors that show us how we are doing when we try to make certain changes, and that when we've learned how to make the changes we don't need the mirrors any more."

It may seem humdrum to use such mental techniques, in the comfort of home or clinic, to achieve lower blood pressure or to overcome common fears and phobias. But there are other, more spectacular applications as well. In his glory days, for example, the daredevil stunt man Evel Knievel piloted his powerful motorcycles into countless situations of heart-stopping danger. It was all in a day's work for Knievel to come roaring out of the wings of Madison Square Garden at seventy miles per hour, zoom up a ramp, fly seventy-five feet through the air, and then land and come to a halt, just before he would have smashed into the other side of the arena. "Life to me is a bore, really," he once quipped, "and jumping has replaced card games, skijumping, stealing."

Millions who watched Knievel in action, either in person or on television, wondered how it was possible for a man to accomplish such astounding stunts. Once, in an interview, Knievel revealed his secret for hurling himself over a lineup of seventeen parked trucks. "I get that motorcycle up there," he said, "and I just see it flying over all those trucks, and landing on the other side."

Knievel was describing a technique called visualization, or imaging. It is used by many athletes and performers, sometimes with the guidance of a psychologist, to visualize—and thus, it is hoped, to manipulate—an upcoming event to obtain the desired outcome. In Soviet Olympic training programs, for example, athletes must develop two skills: the ability to relax the body and put the mind into a calm, receptive state, and the ability to create images of their athletic performances at peak levels and beyond.

This kind of mental rehearsal is called "creative visualization" by some of its devotees. One of them, Shakti Gawain, an avid student of yoga and meditation, has explained how practitioners hope to change the mental image into reality. "The idea is like a blueprint," she says. "It creates an image of the form, which then magnetizes and guides the physical energy to flow into that form and eventually manifests it on the physical plane."

Seeking to formalize such attempts, an American psychologist, Richard M. Suinn, has devised a type of training called controlled dreaming, in which athletes relax into a state that combines the concentration and imagination of a dream with the control of the waking state. Suinn says the athlete using his method can produce the brain waves needed for the performance by creating, in a sense, the human equivalent of a computer program to guide the event.

Some sports stars, however, seem to favor an opposite variation of this technique, an approach that might be called pessimistic visualization. One of them, the tennis player Billie Jean King, has recalled the time in 1963 when, as a young contender, she played so brilliantly at the prestigious annual tournament at Wimbledon, England, that she reached the finals to meet the top-ranked Margaret Court Smith—only to be defeated. "Margaret deserved to win," King conceded later. "But for some reason, that particular loss to Margaret stayed with me for a long time."

King was able to turn her loss into future victory. "Literally for years afterward," she recalled, "whenever I needed something to psych me up before going out to play, I tried to remember the feelings I had during that match, and the sense of utter desolation and failure I felt when we walked off the court. It wasn't a very good feeling and I didn't want to have to repeat it—ever. It was something to avoid, and the best way to avoid it was to win. Just remembering that day got me through a lot of tough matches in the next few years."

For proponents of creative visualization, all that regret and fear would no doubt be disquieting. Their notion is that people—not just athletes, but everyone—can and should bring about good fortune by focusing on it clearly and making it happen. As Shakti Gawain has put it: "We always attract into our lives whatever we think about the most, believe in most strongly, expect on the deepest levels, and/or imagine most vividly."

Even so, experts say that would-be visualizers should not just skip ahead to the happy conclusion of an upcoming challenge. Confront the obstacles, they caution, and pay attention to how you vanquish them; creative visualization is not a whimsical, wishful reverie but a detailed plan for action and success. "One advantage of visualization," says Frances Meritt Stern, director of the Institute for Behavioral Awareness in Plainfield, New Jersey, "is that you can build into it whatever you need, such as the self-instruction that it's okay to feel anxious, you still can go ahead and give your speech or ask for a raise. You can't visualize every contingency; but when you're generally secure, the unexpected doesn't throw you."

Turning Visions into Reality

Seeing is believing—or so the age-old saying goes. But what of things seen only in the imagination, in the mind's eye? Can belief turn such visions into reality?

In hopes that it can, numerous people turn to a method known as visualization, or imaging, to harness the powers of the mind to control or assist the body. Athletes draw mental pictures of themselves performing at their best, continually rehearsing their visions until they play them out in real life. On a more metaphorical level, cancer patients imagine chemotherapy as a magic elixir flooding their systems and washing away the malignant cells. Still others use visualization to reduce stress or alleviate pain.

Precisely how visualization works remains a subject of conjecture and ongoing clinical research. But the fact that it can be effective in certain situations has been understood intuitively for years. To be sure, imaging is no substitute for reality. The cancer patient can no more give up medical treatment than the athlete can forgo physical training. But many sports psychologists and physicians believe that just as depression or despair can impair performance or recovery, a strong positive visualization can enhance it. Several metaphorical visualizations—some of them examples of typical imaging, others the creation of specific individuals—are depicted on the following pages.

Legs widespread, his open hands held gracefully at the ready, a devotee of kung fu strikes a pose reminiscent of a rampant tiger.

Developed in China in AD 300, this martial art calls for practitioners to pattern themselves on a variety of animals—among them the tiger, monkey, deer, bird, and bear.

Students of kung fu are taught to observe the creatures in zoos or in the wild, then visualize themselves becoming each animal—thinking like it and fighting in its distinctive style. The tiger inspires strong, precise movements and a stealthy stalking close to the ground. In the monkey stance, on the other hand, kung fu practitioners do considerable jumping, while as birds they indulge in high kicks.

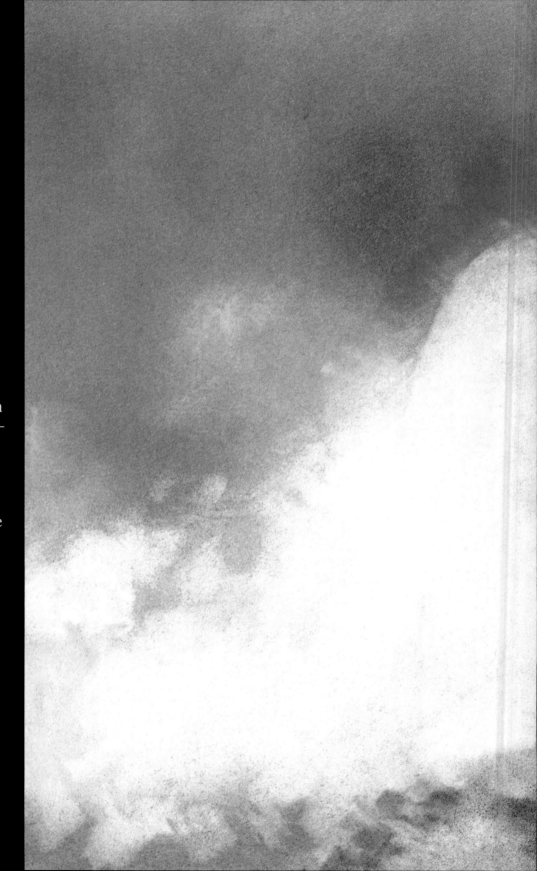

By visualizing a little girl on a playground swing, rhythmically swinging back and forth, a woman is able to bring her irregular heartbeat under control.

In this actual case, visualization may work because the woman's problem is primarily related to anxiety. Increased stress triggers a panic reaction that speeds up her heartbeat. Although not life threatening in itself, the condition is potentially dangerous; she could faint, for example, and strike her head while falling. Instead, whenever she feels stress, she conjures up the little girl on the swing and concentrates on the rhythmic movement.

In need of a burst of energy before she heads onto the ice, a professional skater visualizes herself swallowing a star. It explodes inside her, infusing her with power from the tips of her fingers to her toes.

Athletes have used visualization for years, although their imaging most frequently involves a detailed mental rehearsal of the event—lifting a weight, serving a tennis ball, swinging a golf club—that helps them hold an imaginary practice before the actual competition. In the example shown here, the skater uses the bursting-star image to get the rush of adrenaline she needs to perform at her peak.

A cab driver—a Vietnam veteran who lost a leg in combat—uses visualization to alleviate phantom limb pain. He imagines himself on a beach, watching a sea gull land. As he concentrates on the bird he feels himself becoming the gull and then flying away, leaving his body behind.

Often believed mistakenly to be purely psychosomatic, phantom limb pain is a physical sensation that occurs when nerves once connected to a missing limb continue to transmit signals to the brain. For the disabled veteran, visualization did not eliminate the pain but did help him dissociate himself from it. In addition to focusing on the sea-gull image, he sometimes visualized his painful leg intact and imagined himself treating it with cool cloths and lotions.

A little boy with a malignant brain tumor visualizes video-game rocket ships flying around inside his head and zapping his cancer cells.

Such imagery is often used by young cancer patients; others, preferring less warlike metaphors, visualize their cancer cells being devoured or just carried away. There is no incontrovertible evidence that such imaging can improve a patient's odds for survival. But research in psychoneuroimmunology, a relatively new area of medical inquiry that explores the link between states of mind and the immune system, suggests that visualizing health-promoting images may actually increase the number of white blood cells and other disease-battling body substances.

BIBLIOGRAPHY

"And a Child Shall Lead Them—Astray." *Discover,* May 1984.

Arons, Harry, and Marne F. H. Bubeck, *The Handbook of Professional Hypnosis.* Irvington, N.J.: Power Publishers, 1971.

Bacon, Francis, *The Works of Francis Bacon.* Ed. by James Spedding, Robert Leslie Ellis, and Douglas Denon Heath. Vol. 5. Boston: Houghton, Mifflin, 1900.

Baker, Robert A., "The Aliens among Us: Hypnotic Regression Revisited." *The Skeptical Inquirer,* winter 1987-1988.

Bayless, Raymond, *The Enigma of the Poltergeist.* West Nyack, N.Y.: Parker Publishing, 1967.

Bender, Hans, "Poltergeists." In *Psychical Research: A Guide to Its History, Principles and Practices,* ed. by Ivor Grattan-Guinness. Wellingborough, Northamptonshire, England: Aquarian Press, 1982.

Beyerstein, Barry L.:
"The Brain and Consciousness: Implications for Psi Phenomena." *The Skeptical Inquirer,* winter 1987-1988.
"The Myth of Alpha Consciousness." *The Skeptical Inquirer,* fall 1985.

Bletzer, June G., *The Donning International Encyclopedic Psychic Dictionary.* Norfolk, Va.: Donning Company, 1986.

Bowles, Norma, and Fran Hynds, with Joan Maxwell, *Psi Search.* San Francisco: Harper & Row, 1978.

Bradbury, Will, ed., *Into the Unknown.* Pleasantville, N.Y.: Reader's Digest Association, 1981.

Braud, William, and Marilyn Schlitz, "Psychokinetic Influence on Electrodermal Activity." *The Journal of Parapsychology,* June 1983.

Braude, Stephen E., *ESP and Psychokinesis: A Philosophical Examination.* Philadelphia: Temple University Press, 1979.

Brian, Denis, *The Enchanted Voyager: The Life of J. B. Rhine.* Englewood Cliffs, N.J.: Prentice-Hall, 1982.

Brown, Barbara B., *New Mind, New Body.* New York: Harper & Row, 1974.

Brown, Daniel P., and Erika Fromm, *Hypnotherapy and Hypnoanalysis.* Hillsdale, N.J.: Lawrence Erlbaum Associates, 1986.

Brown, Slater, *The Heyday of Spiritualism.* New York: Hawthorn Books, 1970.

Calkins, Carroll C., ed., *Mysteries of the Unexplained.* Pleasantville, N.Y.: Reader's Digest Association, 1982.

"Can Mind Affect Body Defenses against Disease?" *Journal of the American Medical Association,* July 18, 1986.

Carrington, Hereward, *Eusapia Palladino and Her Phenomena.* New York: B. W. Dodge, 1909.

Cavendish, Richard, ed., *Man, Myth & Magic.* New York: Marshall Cavendish, 1983.

Chauvin, Rémy, *Parapsychology: When the Irrational Rejoins Science.* Trans. by Katharine M. Banham. Jefferson, N.C.: McFarland, 1985.

Cheek, David B., and Leslie M. LeCron, *Clinical Hypnotherapy.* New York: Grune & Stratton, 1968.

Christie-Murray, David:
"Other Voices, Other Lives." *The Unexplained* (London), Vol. 2, Issue 3.
"Tomorrow and Tomorrow." *The Unexplained* (London), Vol. 6, Issue 69.

Clark, A. V., *Psycho-Kinesis: Moving Matter with the Mind.* West Nyack, N.Y.: Parker Publishing, 1973.

Cole, T. C., Jr., *Prof. T. C. Cole's Jr. Complete Mail Course in Hypnotism: Twenty-Five Illustrated Lessons.* Jonesboro, Ark., 1900.

Corrick, James A., *The Human Brain: Mind and Matter.* New York: Arco Publishing, 1983.

Council on Scientific Affairs, "Scientific Status of Refreshing Recollection by the Use of Hypnosis." *Journal of the American Medical Association,* April 5, 1985.

Dennett, Michael R., "Firewalking: Reality or Illusion?" *The Skeptical Inquirer,* fall 1985.

Doherty, Jim, "Hot Feat: Firewalkers of the World." *Science Digest,* August 1982.

Dougherty, Pat, "Gilda." *Life Magazine,* March 1988.

Druckman, Daniel, and John A. Swets, eds., *Enhancing Human Performance: Issues, Theories, and Techniques.* Washington, D.C.: National Academy of Sciences, 1988.

Early, L. F., and J. E. Lifschutz, "A Case of Stigmata." *Archives of General Psychiatry,* February 1974.

Ebon, Martin, *Psychic Warfare: Threat or Illusion?* New York: McGraw-Hill, 1983.

Edmonston, William E., Jr., *The Induction of Hypnosis.* New York: John Wiley & Sons, 1986.

Eisenbud, Jule, *The World of Ted Serios.* New York: William Morrow, 1967.

Ellenberger, Henri F., *The Discovery of the Unconscious.* New York: Basic Books, 1970.

Elliott, Richard, *The Competitive Edge: Mental Preparation for Distance Running.* Englewood Cliffs, N.J.: Prentice-Hall, 1984.

Erickson, Milton H.:
Advanced Techniques of Hypnosis and Therapy: Selected Papers of Milton H. Erickson, M.D. Ed. by Jay Haley. New York: Grune & Stratton, 1967.
Healing in Hypnosis. Ed. by Ernest L. Rossi, Margaret O. Ryan, and Florence A. Sharp. Vol. 1. New York: Irvington Publishers with New Horizon Press, 1983.

Eysenck, Hans J., and Carl Sargent, *Explaining the Unexplained: Mysteries of the Paranormal.* London: Weidenfeld and Nicolson, 1982.

Fairley, John, and Simon Welfare, *Arthur C. Clarke's World of Strange Powers.* New York: G. P. Putnam's Sons, 1984.

Flammarion, Camille, *Mysterious Psychic Forces.* Boston: Small, Maynard, 1907.

Forem, Jack, *Transcendental Meditation: Maharishi Mahesh Yogi and the Science of Creative Intelligence.* New York: E. P. Dutton, 1974.

Gardner, Martin:
"Geller, Gulls, and Nitinol." *The Humanist,* May-June 1977.
"Parapsychology and Quantum Mechanics." In *Science and the Paranormal,* ed. by George O. Abell and Barry Singer. New York: Scribner's, 1983.

Garfield, Charles A., with Hal Zina Bennett, *Peak Performance: Mental Training Techniques of the World's Greatest Athletes.* New York: Warner Books, 1984.

Garrison, Peter, "Kindling Courage." *Omni,* April 1985.

Gauld, Alan, and A. D. Cornell, *Poltergeists.* London: Routledge & Kegan Paul, 1979.

Geller, Uri, *My Story.* New York: Praeger, 1975.

Geller, Uri, and Guy Lyon Playfair, *The Geller Effect.* London: Jonathan Cape, 1986.

Godman, Colin, and Lindsay St. Claire, "A Spirit of Anger." *The Unexplained* (London), Vol. 7, Issue 79.

Green, Elmer, and Alyce Green, *Beyond Biofeedback.* New York: Merloyd Lawrence, 1977.

Haley, Jay, *Uncommon Therapy: The Psychiatric Techniques of Milton H. Erickson, M.D.* New York: W. W. Norton, 1973.

Hall, Trevor H., *The Enigma of Daniel Home: Medium or Fraud?* Buffalo, N.Y.: Prometheus Books, 1984.

Hallander, Jane, *Kung Fu Fighting Styles.* Burbank, Calif.: Unique Publications, 1985.

Hansel, C. E. M., *ESP and Parapsychology: A Critical Reevaluation.* Buffalo, N.Y.: Prometheus Books, 1980.

Harris, Melvin:
"Life before Life?" *The Unexplained* (London), Vol. 11, Issue 132.
"Plumbing the Depths." *The Unexplained* (London), Vol. 11, Issue 131.

Hasted, John, *The Metal-Benders.* London: Routledge & Kegan Paul, 1981.

Hilgard, Ernest R., and Josephine R. Hilgard, *Hypnosis in the Relief of Pain.* Los Altos, Calif.: William Kaufmann, 1983.

Hill, Scott, "The Psychokinetic Phenomena of Nina Kulagina." *Fate,* August 1986.

Hines, Terence, *Pseudoscience and the Paranormal.* Buffalo, N.Y.: Prometheus Books, 1988.

Holroyd, Stuart, *Minds without Boundaries.* Garden City, N.Y.: Doubleday, 1976.

Hull, Clark L., *Hypnosis and Suggestibility.* New York: Appleton-Century-Crofts, 1968.

Inglis, Brian:
"The Power of Suggestion." *The Unexplained* (London), Vol. 2, Issue 1.
Science and Parascience: A History of the Paranormal, 1914-1939. London: Hodder and Stoughton, 1984.

Isaacs, Julian, "Now You See It . . ." *The Unexplained* (London), Vol. 12, Issue 135.

Jahn, Robert G., and Brenda J. Dunne, "On the Quantum Mechanics of Consciousness, with Application to Anomalous Phenomena." *Foundations of Physics,* August 1986.

Karlins, Marvin, and Lewis M. Andrews, *Biofeedback: Turning on the Power of Your Mind.* Philadelphia: J. B. Lippincott, 1972.

Kelly, Sean F., and Reid J. Kelly, *Hypnosis: Understanding How It Can Work for You.* Reading, Mass.: Addison-Wesley, 1985.

Khim, P'ng Chye, and Donn F. Draeger, *Shaolin: An Introduction to Lohan Fighting Techniques.* Rutland, Vt.: Charles E. Tuttle, 1979.

Kline, Milton V., *Freud and Hypnosis: The Interaction of Psychodynamics and Hypnosis.* New York: Julian Press, 1958.

Krier, Beth Ann, "The Curious Hotfoot It to a New Fad." *Los Angeles Times,* April 11, 1984.

Krippner, Stanley, ed., *Advances in Parapsychological Research.* Vol. 1. New York: Plenum Press, 1977. Vol. 5. Jefferson, N.C.: McFarland, 1987.

Laurence, Jean-Roch, and Campbell Perry, *Hypnosis, Will, and Memory: A Psycho-Legal History.* New York: Guilford Press, 1988.

LeCron, Leslie M., *Self Hypnotism.* New York: New American Library, 1964.

LeCron, Leslie M., ed., *Experimental Hypnosis.* New York: Macmillan, 1952.

Leikind, Bernard J., and William J. McCarthy, "An Investigation of Firewalking." *The Skeptical Inquirer,* fall 1985.

LeRoy, Olivier, *Levitation: An Examination of the Evidence and Explanations.* London: Burns, Oates & Washbourne, 1928.

Locke, Steven, and Douglas Colligan, *The Healer within: The New Medicine of Mind and Body.* New York: E. P. Dutton, 1986.

McConkey, Kevin M., and Campbell Perry, "Benjamin Franklin and Mesmerism." *The International Journal of Clinical and Experimental Hypnosis,* April 1985.

Mackenzie, Andrew, "Witness to the Unexplained." *Shef-*

field Morning Telegraph, November 29, 1965.

McRae, Ronald M., *Mind Wars: The True Story of Government Research into the Military Potential of Psychic Weapons.* New York: St. Martin's Press, 1984.

"Meditation and Sleep." *Science News,* January 24, 1976.

Monaghan, Frank J., *Hypnosis in Criminal Investigation.* Dubuque, Iowa: Kendall/Hunt, 1980.

Morgan, George E., M.D., *Hypnosis in Ophthalmology.* Birmingham, Ala.: Aesculapius, 1980.

Murphy, Michael, and Rhea A. White, *The Psychic Side of Sports.* Reading, Mass.: Addison-Wesley, 1978.

Murphy, Wendy, and the Editors of Time-Life Books, *Dealing with Headaches* (Library of Health series). Alexandria, Va.: Time-Life Books, 1982.

Ormond, Leonée, *George Du Maurier.* London: Routledge & Kegan Paul, 1969.

Orne, Martin T., "The Mechanisms of Hypnotic Age Regression: An Experimental Study." *The Journal of Abnormal and Social Psychology,* April 1951.

Orne, Martin T., David F. Dinges, and Emily Carota Orne, "The Forensic Use of Hypnosis." *Research in Brief* (The National Institute of Justice), December 1984.

Ostrander, Shelia, and Lynn Schroeder, *Psychic Discoveries behind the Iron Curtain.* Englewood Cliffs, N.J.: Prentice-Hall, 1970.

Owen, A. R. G., *Can We Explain the Poltergeist?* New York: Garrett Publications, 1964.

Owen, Iris M., *Conjuring Up Philip: An Adventure in Psychokinesis.* Toronto: Fitzhenry & Whiteside, 1976.

Pagels, Heinz R., *The Cosmic Code: Quantum Physics As the Language of Nature.* New York: Simon and Schuster, 1982.

Pratt, J. G., and W. G. Roll, "The Seaford Disturbances." *The Journal of Parapsychology,* June 1958.

Price, Harry:
Rudi Schneider: A Scientific Examination of His Mediumship. London: Methuen, no date.
Stella C.: A Page of Psychic History. London: John M. Watkins, 1924.

Puharich, Andrija, *Uri: A Journal of the Mystery of Uri Geller.* Garden City, N.Y.: Doubleday, 1974.

Randall, John L., *Psychokinesis: A Study of Paranormal Forces through the Ages.* London: Souvenir Press, 1982.

Randi, James:
Flim-Flam! Buffalo, N.Y.: Prometheus Books, 1982.
The Truth about Uri Geller. Buffalo, N.Y.: Prometheus Books, 1982.

Reiser, Martin, *Handbook of Investigative Hypnosis.* Los Angeles, Calif.: LEHI Publishing, 1980.

Reveen, Peter J., "Fantasizing Under Hypnosis: Some Experimental Evidence." *The Skeptical Inquirer,* winter 1987-1988.

Rhine, Louisa E.:
Mind over Matter: Psychokinesis. New York: Macmillan, 1970.
Something Hidden. Jefferson, N.C.: McFarland, 1983.

Richards, John Thomas, *SORRAT: A History of the Neihardt Psychokinesis Experiments, 1961-1981.* Metuchen, N.J.: Scarecrow Press, 1982.

Richards, Steve, *Levitation: What It Is-How It Works-How to Do It.* Wellingborough, Northamptonshire, England: Aquarian Press, 1980.

Richet, Charles, *Thirty Years of Psychical Research.* Trans. by Stanley De Brath. New York: Macmillan, 1923.

Robbins, Rossell Hope, *The Encyclopedia of Witchcraft and Demonology.* New York: Bonanza Books, 1981.

Robinson, Diana, *To Stretch a Plank: A Survey of Psychokinesis.* Chicago: Nelson-Hall, 1981.

Robinson, Richard, *Kung Fu: The Peaceful Way.* New York: Pyramid Books, 1974.

Rogo, D. Scott:
Mind over Matter: The Case for Psychokinesis. Wellingborough, Northamptonshire, England: Aquarian Press, 1986.
Minds and Motion: The Riddle of Psychokinesis. New York: Taplinger, 1978.
The Poltergeist Experience. Harmondsworth, Middlesex, England: Penguin Books, 1979.

Roll, W. G., *The Poltergeist.* Metuchen, N.J.: Scarecrow Press, 1976.

Roll, W. G., and J. G. Pratt, "The Miami Disturbances." *The Journal of the American Society for Psychical Research,* October 1971.

Sarbin, Theodore R., and William C. Coe, *Hypnosis: A Social Psychological Analysis of Influence Communication.* New York: Holt, Rinehart and Winston, 1972.

Schmeidler, Gertrude R., "PK Effects upon Continuously Recorded Temperature." *The Journal of the American Society for Psychical Research,* October 1973.

Schmeidler, Gertrude R., ed., *Parapsychology: Its Relation to Physics, Biology, Psychology, and Psychiatry.* Metuchen, N.J.: Scarecrow Press, 1976.

Schmidt, Helmut:
"PK Effect on Pre-Recorded Targets." *The Journal of the American Society for Psychical Research,* July 1976.
"Psychokinesis." In *Psychic Exploration: A Challenge for Science,* ed. by Edgar D. Mitchell. New York: G. P. Putnam's Sons, 1974.

Schrey, Carola, *Die Wahrheit über den Spukfall am Chiemsee.* Wiesbaden, Germany: Credo Verlag, 1950.

Sheehan, Peter W., and Campbell W. Perry, *Methodologies of Hypnosis: A Critical Appraisal of Contemporary Paradigms of Hypnosis.* Hillsdale, N.J.: Lawrence Erlbaum, 1976.

Shepard, Leslie A., ed., *Encyclopedia of Occultism & Para-*

psychology. Vols. 1 and 3. Detroit, Mich.: Gale Research, 1985.

Shore, Steven N., "Quantum Theory and the Paranormal: The Misuse of Science." *The Skeptical Inquirer,* fall 1984.

Siegel, Bernie S., *Love, Medicine & Miracles.* New York: Harper & Row, 1986.

Silva, José, and Philip Miele. *The Silva Mind Control Method.* New York: Pocket Books, 1977.

Simonton, O. Carl, Stephanie Matthews-Simonton, and James Creighton. *Getting Well Again.* Los Angeles: J. P. Tarcher, 1978.

Smyth, Frank, "The Mastery of Fire." *The Unexplained* (London), Vol. 2, Issue 17.

Spanos, Nicholas P., "Past-Life Regression: A Critical View." *The Skeptical Inquirer,* winter 1987-1988.

Squires, Sally, "Visions to Boost Immunity." *American Health,* July-August 1987.

Swann, Ingo, *To Kiss Earth Good-Bye.* New York: Hawthorn Books, 1975.

Targ, Russell, and Harold E. Puthoff, *Mind-Reach.* New York: Delacorte Press, 1977.

Taylor, John, *Superminds.* London: Macmillan, 1975.

Teich, Mark, and Giselle Dodeles, "Mind Control: How to Get It, How to Use It, How to Keep It." *Omni,* October-December 1987.

Tinterow, Maurice M., *Foundations of Hypnosis.* Springfield, Ill.: Charles C. Thomas, 1970.

"TM's Claims Unsupported in Experiments." *Science Digest,* August 1977.

Tompkins, Peter, and Christopher Bird, *The Secret Life of Plants.* New York: Harper & Row, 1973.

Udolf, Roy, *Handbook of Hypnosis for Professionals.* New York: Van Nostrand Reinhold, 1987.

Walker, Jearl, "Drops of Water Dance on a Hot Skillet and the Experimenter Walks on Hot Coals." *Scientific American,* August 1977.

Watson, Lyall, *Lifetide: A Biology of the Unconscious.* London: Hodder and Stoughton, 1979.

Weiner, Debra H., and Dean I. Radin, eds., *Research in Parapsychology 1985.* Metuchen, N.J.: Scarecrow Press, 1986.

Wiene, Robert, Carl Mayer, and Hans Janowitz, *The Cabinet of Dr. Caligari* (film). Script translation and description of action by R. V. Adkinson. London: Lorrimer Publishing, 1972.

Wilson, Colin, *The Geller Phenomenon.* London: Danbury Press, 1976.

Wilson, Ian, *All in the Mind.* Garden City, N.Y.: Doubleday, 1982.

Witherow, John, and Jon Connell, "Did Uri Bend the Will of Gorbachev?" *The Sunday Times* (London), May 3, 1987.

Wolman, Benjamin, ed., *Handbook of Parapsychology.* New York: Van Nostrand Reinhold, 1977.

PICTURE CREDITS

ACKNOWLEDGMENTS

The editors wish to thank the following individuals and institutions for their valuable assistance in the preparation of this volume: Archana, Yoga Research Foundation, Miami, Florida; Professor Hans Bender, Institut für Grenzgebiete der Psychologie und Psychohygiene, Freiburg, West Germany; Barry Beyerstein, Department of Psychology, Simon Frazer University, Burnaby, British Columbia, Canada; Nicholas Clark-Lowes, London; Hilary Evans, London; Federazione Italiana Sport Handicappati, Rome; Leif Geiges, Staufen, West Germany; Uri Geller, Berkshire, England; Istituto Scienza dello Sport, Rome; Heidi Klein, Bildarchiv Preussischer Kulturbesitz; Gabrielle Kohler-Gallei, Archiv für kunst und Geschichte, West Berlin; Dr. Wolfgang Larbig, Psychologisches Institut, Universität Tübingen, Tübingen, West Germany; Professor Johannes Mischo, Institut für Psychologie und Grenzgebiete der Psychologie, Universität Freiburg, Freiburg, West Germany; Professor Claudio Modigliani, Rome; Eleanor O'Keeffe, London; Martin Orne, Unit for Experimental Psychiatry, Philadelphia, Pennsylvania; Dr. Oscar Ratnoff, University Hospitals of Cleveland, Ohio; D. Scott Rogo, Northridge, California; Bernard Rudolph, Tübingen, West Germany; Shipi Shtrang, Berkshire, England; Dr. Rolf Streichardt, Institut für Grenzgebiete der Psychologie und Psychohygiene, Freiburg, West Germany; Jean Watelet, Conservateur Département des Périodiques, Bibliothèque Nationale, Paris; Alan Wesencraft, Harry Price Library, University of London.

INDEX

Time-Life Books Inc.
is a wholly owned subsidiary of
TIME INCORPORATED

FOUNDER: Henry R. Luce 1898-1967

Editor-in-Chief: Jason McManus
Chairman and Chief Executive Officer: J. Richard Munro
President and Chief Operating Officer: N. J. Nicholas, Jr.
Editorial Director: Ray Cave
Executive Vice President, Books: Kelso F. Sutton
Vice President, Books: George Artandi

TIME-LIFE BOOKS INC.

EDITOR: George Constable
Executive Editor: Ellen Phillips
Director of Design: Louis Klein
Director of Editorial Resources: Phyllis K. Wise
Editorial Board: Russell B. Adams, Jr., Dale M. Brown,
Roberta Conlan, Thomas H. Flaherty, Lee Hassig, Donia
Ann Steele, Rosalind Stubenberg, Henry Woodhead
Director of Photography and Research:
John Conrad Weiser
Assistant Director of Editorial Resources: Elise Ritter Gibson

PRESIDENT: Christopher T. Linen
Chief Operating Officer: John M. Fahey, Jr.
Senior Vice Presidents: Robert M. DeSena, James L. Mercer,
Paul R. Stewart
Vice Presidents: Stephen L. Bair, Ralph J. Cuomo, Neal
Goff, Stephen L. Goldstein, Juanita T. James, Hallett
Johnson III, Carol Kaplan, Susan J. Maruyama, Robert H.
Smith, Joseph J. Ward
Director of Production Services: Robert J. Passantino

Editorial Operations
Copy Chief: Diane Ullius
Production: Celia Beattie
Library: Louise D. Forstall

Library of Congress Cataloging in Publication Data
Mind over matter/the editors of Time-Life Books.
    p. cm.—(Mysteries of the unknown)
    Bibliography: p.
    Includes index.
    ISBN 0-8094-6336-9. ISBN 0-8094-6337-7 (lib. bdg.)
    1. Psychokinesis. I. Time-Life Books. II. Series.
    BF1371.M55 1988
    133.8'8—dc19   88-12338 CIP

MYSTERIES OF THE UNKNOWN

SERIES DIRECTOR: Russell B. Adams, Jr.
Series Administrator: Myrna Traylor-Herndon
Designer: Susan K. White

Editorial Staff for *Mind over Matter*
Associate Editors: Scarlet Cheng, Jane N. Coughran
(pictures); Janet P. Cave (text)
Writers: Janet P. Cave, Laura Foreman
Assistant Designer: Lorraine D. Rivard
Copy Coordinator: Mary Beth Oelkers-Keegan
Picture Coordinators: Adrienne L. Szafran, Betty H.
Weatherley
Researchers: Christian D. Kinney, Sharon Obermiller, Paula
Y. Soderlund, Connie Contreras, Elizabeth Ward
Editorial Assistant: Donna Fountain

Special Contributors: Christine Hinze (London, picture
research); Patricia A. Paterno (pictures); Amy G. Aldrich,
Sarah Brash, William F. Heavey, Peter Kaufman,
Martha Leff, Valerie Moolman, Wendy Murphy, Sandra
Salmans, Daniel M. Stashower, David S. Thomson (text);
John Drummond (design); John L. Dodge, Roxie France-
Nuriddin, (research); Jane B. Clark (copyediting); Hazel
Blumberg-McKee (index)
Correspondents: Elisabeth Kraemer-Singh (Bonn), Vanessa
Kramer (London), Maria Vincenza Aloisi (Paris), Ann
Natanson (Rome)
Valuable assistance was also provided by Judy Aspinall
(London); Arti Ahluwalia (New Delhi); Elizabeth Brown,
Christina Lieberman (New York); Ann Wise (Rome); Dick
Berry, Mieko Ikeda (Tokyo)

The Consultants:
Dr. Stanley N. Chase, contributor to the essay on
self-hypnosis, is a clinical psychologist currently practicing in Bethesda, Maryland. He has specialized in the
application of hypnosis to the areas of habit control,
phobia treatment, stress reduction, and neurotic disorders, and his latest research is concerned with techniques
and applications of self-hypnosis.

William G. Roll, professor of psychology and psychical
research at West Georgia College, is project director of the
Psychical Research Foundation, an independent research
and educational organization founded at Duke University.
He has investigated cases of recurrent spontaneous
psychokinesis and is the author of *The Poltergeist.* He has
also written numerous articles on and made many
contributions to the subject of psychokinesis.

Marcello Truzzi, professor of sociology at Eastern
Michigan University, is also director of the Center for
Scientific Anomalies Research (CSAR) and editor of its
journal, the *Zetetic Scholar.* Dr. Truzzi, who considers
himself a "constructive skeptic" with regard to claims of
the paranormal, works through the CSAR to produce
dialogues between critics and proponents of unusual
scientific claims.

Other Publications:

AMERICAN COUNTRY
VOYAGE THROUGH THE UNIVERSE
THE THIRD REICH
THE TIME-LIFE GARDENER'S GUIDE
TIME FRAME
FIX IT YOURSELF
FITNESS, HEALTH & NUTRITION
SUCCESSFUL PARENTING
HEALTHY HOME COOKING
UNDERSTANDING COMPUTERS
LIBRARY OF NATIONS
THE ENCHANTED WORLD
THE KODAK LIBRARY OF CREATIVE PHOTOGRAPHY
GREAT MEALS IN MINUTES
THE CIVIL WAR
PLANET EARTH
COLLECTOR'S LIBRARY OF THE CIVIL WAR
THE EPIC OF FLIGHT
THE GOOD COOK
WORLD WAR II
HOME REPAIR AND IMPROVEMENT
THE OLD WEST

*For information on and a full description of any of the
Time-Life Books series listed above, please call 1-800-
621-7026 or write:*
    Reader Information
    Time-Life Customer Service
    P.O. Box C-32068
    Richmond, Virginia 23261-2068

This volume is one of a series that examines the history
and nature of seemingly paranormal phenomena. Other
books in the series include:
Mystic Places
Psychic Powers
The UFO Phenomenon
Psychic Voyages
Phantom Encounters
Visions and Prophecies
Mysterious Creatures

TIME
LIFE ®